The Life and Times of Perley the Magician

Tributes and stories from family, friends, and colleagues gathered by Perly Palmer; his wife, Valerie; and Dr. Bonnie.

Collaborated and Edited by:
Bonnie M. Clark Douglass, EdD

Strategic Book Publishing and Rights Co.

Copyright © 2017 Bonnie Clark Douglass, EdD. All rights reserved.

No part of this book may be reproduced or transmitted in any form or by any means, graphic, electronic, or mechanical, including photocopying, recording, taping, or by any information storage retrieval system, without the permission, in writing, of the publisher.

Strategic Book Publishing and Rights Co.
USA | Singapore
www.sbpra.com

ISBN: 978-1-68181-924-2

Cover Design: Peggy Ann Rupp, Dedicated Book Services

Book Design: Dedicated Book Services

Dedication

*This book is being dedicated to my mother, Edith;
my beautiful wife, Valerie, and our family and friends.*

Perley and Valerie
Young Love

Perley and Valerie
at their Wedding

Perley and his Mom
2016.

Mom is still living and is 92 now. I love her so much. I just came back from visiting her in a nursing home in Victoria, British Columbia. I am so grateful that I was able to spend time with her in October, 2016. I held her and told her I loved her. It's funny we held on to each other so closely it was as if we both knew that was the last time we would look into each other's eyes.

"Before I created you in the womb, I knew you; before you were born; I set you apart. I made you a prophet to the nations."

Jeremiah 1:5 (CEB)

Table of Contents

Acknowledgments 1
From Editor Bonnie Clark Douglass, EdD 3
Introduction 4
Tribute and Insight by Gordon Burtt 5
Staff Sgt. Paul Babtiste Tribute 6
Tribute from Mayor Brad Woodside 7
Tribute to Perley the Magician—Mike Vokey,
    Executive Director, Fredericton Exhibition 8
Tribute to Perley the Magician—Peter and Janet Clark,
    Jellystone Park, Woodstock, NB 9
Tribute to Perley the Magician—Brent Buchanan,
    Morning Host Country KHJ 10
Introducing Perley 11
My Memory About Perley's Birth by Louise 'Weezie'
    Duncan 13
My Earliest Memories in Doaktown 15
Bubby Dayton Recollections 18
Perley's Memories 19
A Few Stories by Barry Sullivan 23
Perley's Friends and Fun 25
Charlie Hickey's Memories 26
Perley and School 27
Tribute From Allison Kingston 28
Life Moved on 29
Memories From Larry Ackerson 30
Perley's Journey 32
Another Vivid Memory From Charlie Hickey 33
My Teens and New Adventures 34

Tribute by Alan Lyons 39
A Tribute and a Memory by Nephew Doug Duncan—Weezie's Son . 41
Life Moved Forward. 42
Tribute by Richard Tingley 45
Becoming a Magician 48
Some of the Things I Remember About my Best Friend,
    Perley Palmer 50
Perley's Family Life and the Changes 52
Perley and Valerie Meet: Our First Meeting—by Valerie Palmer . . . 53
Perley Takes a Risk. 54
Our First Date-Valerie 55
How Holly Helped Perley 56
Perley and the Blended Family 58
June 2, 1984: Perley and Valerie's Wedding Day-
    Valerie Gives the Details 59
The Honeymoon 60
Perley's Desire to Become a Magician Grows 61
Magic by Janelle Peters 62
Perley's Magic Spreading. 63
The Magician's Tributes 65
Tribute From Magician Brent Cairns. 67
Tribute From Magician Chris Lovely. 68
A Tribute From Mike D'Urzo-Mega Magic. 69
A Tribute From David Johnson, the Magician. 70
Perley Concludes. 71
A Tribute to Perley Palmer-Dow Johnston 72
Tributes: The Many Friends and Businesses and Colleagues of
    Perley, the Magician. 74
Fredericton City Police Force 74
    -Leanne J. Fitch, Chief of Police/Chef de Police M.O.M. 74
    -Staff Sergeant Paul Babtiste 75
    -Karla Forsythe. 77

- The Character of Our Friend, Perley Palmer: Tribute by Steve, Karen, Amber, and Chelsea Cliff. 77
- Andrew Frizzell, Age 7 77
- Jerett Blackmore 77
- Bruce, Age 9 78
- Ben, Age 8 78
- Lily, Age 4 78
- Tribute From Denis Vanember 78
- Tribute From Scott Patterson 78
- Andrew Miller, 50 79
- Judy McCarty 79
- Olivia Babtiste, Age 10 79
- Hannah Babtiste, Age 13 79

A Tribute From Brookside Mall Property Manager, Tim Woods.... 80

A Tribute From Jellystone Park NB: Janet and Peter Clark. 81

The FREX 82

A Tribute to my Friend, Perley, the Magician: Mike Vokey 83

A Tribute From Tim Gillies 85

A Tribute From Gary Gordon 86

Perley Reflects 88

Meeting the Mayor 89

Tribute From Brad Woodside 90

Proclamation Day 91

Perley Palmer Day 93

Our Community 95

Life Changes—Owen Brewer–Memories 96

Retiring 98

Cancer Diagnosis 99

Valerie Recalls the Cancer Diagnosis on April 1, 2015 100

Perley Moves Forward 101

A Loving Tribute From Amy Lee Doucette 102

Perley Reflects **104**
Tribute From Family Members **106**
   -From Doug Duncan 106
   -Memories of my Brother, Perley: Roger Palmer 106
   -Memories of Perley by Brother Ivan 109
   -Message From Kelly Palmer, Kim, Perley's Youngest Daughter 111
   -A Tribute to my Dad From Faye............................. 113
   -From Perley's Only Son, Michael............................ 115
   -Tribute From Pastor Theo Craig............................. 119
   -Tribute to my Dad, Perley the Magician: Pat Price............... 121
Experiencing Generosity... **123**
Our Blessings—Valerie **124**
Tribute by Dave-RV World **125**
"Dr. Bonnie" Reflects... **126**
A Lifelong Lesson Learned: Michael Palmer.................. **127**
Dreams Come True: Facing Life Hand in Hand—Valerie **128**
Conclusion **129**
References **131**

Acknowledgments

Perley, the Magician

It seems fitting that I give special thanks to my good friend, Bob Dewar, for lighting the match that lit the candle and revealed the path to create this book and my legacy that will endure for all time.

First and foremost, I would like to thank God for being ever present in my life. I am so grateful for my beautiful wife, Valerie, and my mom for being by my side and supporting my dreams. I would like to thank our children, Faye, Kelly, Michael, Pat, and Theo; and our grandchildren for being an important part of my life. My brothers, Roger and Ivan, have walked life's journey with me and I am forever grateful to have them and their families as part of my life. I would like to remember "Nan" Ruby for helping to shape my life, and my "special" sister, Weezie (Louise) Duncan, for being forever present.

Mr. Bob Dewar - Owner of Dairy Queen Brazier of Fredericton, NB. Major Sponsor of Perley's book.

I would like to say "thank you" to all of the contributors and friends that I have shared much of my life with: Sobeys, Tingleys, Richard Tingley, Nashwaaksis Save Easy, St. Mary's Supermarket, Fredericton Police Force, Brad Woodside, Fredericton Exhibition staff, Mike Vokey, Brookside Mall staff, Tim Wood, Brent Buchanan, Larry Ackerson, Owen Brewer, Tim Gillies, Charlie Hickey, Barry Sullivan, Dow Johnston, Alison Kingston, Irving Pulp and Paper Company, Gordon Burtt, Gary Gordon, RV World, and all my wonderful friends. Thanks to "my girl," Amy, and many like Amy who have the faith and courage to believe in magic.

Special thanks for the opportunity of being at many day cares, events at Jellystone Park, birthdays, and other events covered by *The Daily Gleaner*, *The Telegraph Journal*, CJRI, KHJ, and CBC.

Thank you to the many magicians who have helped shape my career in magic. I want to express my gratitude for the magician conventions, workshops, and the excellent work they all do to help magicians develop so we, in turn, can make the world a happier place to live. Thank you to

Magicians June Lamb, Brent Cairns, Chris Lovely, Mike D'Urzo, and Dave Johnson are included and appreciated. Thank you to the friends and family who submitted photos–Richard Tingley, Billy Hanson, Bill Saunders, and many family members. Thanks to Strategic Publishing staff that expedited the production of the book.

My good friend, Bob Dewar, entrepreneur and owner of the local Dairy Queen, is the major sponsor of this book, along with Positive Heart Living. Thank you for making my dream a reality.

Special thanks to Dr. Bonnie who collaborated my book, guided me, gathered tributes, and for writing my story. Thanks to Shirley V. Duncan, from Sarasota, Florida, Leah Butler and Lucas Tapley for assisted editing. Special thanks to Heather Slowski, from Nanaimo, BC, for her professional editing skills and helping to complete the book for all my loved ones.

Love Purley

From Editor
Bonnie Clark Douglass, EdD

Positive Heart Living has always taken a leap of faith into any opportunity, when asked, to help someone make the world a better place–and Perley is one of those people. It is a blessing and an honour to be part of Perley's life through our personal conversations, connection with his family, and Perley's so many "best friends," business leaders, and magicians. After all, anyone who has a day named after him by his city has obviously been a servant to all–and that has always been Perley's calling, which is revealed throughout his amazing story.

Rt. Dr. Everett Chalmers Co-Founder of Positive Heart Living, Middle Dr. Bonnie-Founder-Long time volunteer Joan Manzer

Introduction

A group of Perley's friends got together and the idea of having Perley Palmer's story written and his amazing journey told was the outcome of their round-table coffee discussion. Here we are—thanks to his family, best friends, community members, people of the province, and a world of individuals who have and will fall in love with Perley.

Tribute and Insight by Gordon Burtt

One late summer morning, I was in a local establishment sipping a hot beverage when a lady entered with several children in tow. After ordering lunch, they settled into a seating area to enjoy their booty, except for one boy who made a project of eyeballing a curly-haired occupant of a nearby booth. I heard him yell, "Mom, I know that guy!" Unable to contain himself any longer, the young lad approached the icon, exclaiming in an uncontainable outburst, "I know who you are!" The curly-haired man turned with a big smile and responded with a rousing, "And I know who you are!" There then ensued a spellbinding period where all present were treated to a performance by this notorious magician. It was truly mesmerizing!

Perley Palmer was working his magic once again. I watched for about my one-hundredth time at the hypnotic effect he had on children of all ages. I was convinced of the true magic of this performance, which was also revealed in the eyes of the children and all of us watching. It was evident there was a life to explore, a story that must be told about the journey that brought Perley the Magician to this place and time. It is time to share with all who know and love him, and those that will once they engage in his magical life journey.

Your friend,
Gordon Burtt

Staff Sgt. Paul Babtiste Tribute-FPF

Perley, you are a true man, a true inspiration, a mentor—someone who throughout your life has impacted so many in a positive way. If the rest of us could only learn to practice a portion of what you represent and your true desire to be there for others, this world would be a better place to live. Take care of yourself, my friend. I look forward to many more tricks from you!

With great respect,
Paul

Fredericton Police Force Officers with Perley–Paul Battiste left, Steve Cliff right.

Tribute from Mayor Brad Woodside

Brad Woodside

Perley has a real connection with people. I can't even imagine the number of birthday parties and magic shows Perley has done, but I'm sure it is a lot. When Perley was having health challenges, I thought it would be appropriate to have a special day set aside to honor Perley for the wonderful support he has given our communities for so long. It is an opportunity for a lot of us to say, "Thanks; you're magical and loved by a lot of people."

                      Your friend,
                      Brad

Tribute to Perley the Magician—Mike Vokey, Executive Director, Fredericton Exhibition

To be recognized and appreciated in the community is a wonderful achievement. To be known for your talent as an entertainer and for the joy and laughter you bring to others is a blessing. To be acknowledged for the lifetime of contributions in the community and by the community is humbling. This is not a story about a great magician. This is a story about a great man.

Perley at FREX- 2015.

Tribute to Perley the Magician—Peter and Janet Clark, Jellystone Park, Woodstock, NB

Perley is truly a "one of a kind" and he always puts one hundred ten percent into everything he does! This is why we made him an honorary Park Ranger and now we affectionately call him "Ranger Perley!"

Perley and Yogi Bear.

Tribute to Perley the Magician—Brent Buchanan, Morning Host Country KHJ

Brent Buchanan and Perley

If Perley was paid in smiles, he would have been a millionaire a long, long time ago. Perley has put smiles on so many faces over the years, both young and old. When my daughter, Emma, was young, she would literally push me out of the way to get to Perley. Perley might be in the middle of a conversation with one of his many friends at the local markets, Fredericton Exhibition, or a grocery store, but when one of his fans tugs on his shirt, he always stops what he is doing to pull a red ball out of their ear or yank a coin out of their nose. I know he loves it, as much as the kids do. I have been fortunate to meet many interesting and talented people over the years, but none as magical as my friend, Perley.

We love you, Perly!
Brent

James Buchanan, 3rd Annual Perly Palmer Day

Brent and his children, James and Emma

Introducing Perley

My name is Perley Palmer and I was born on February 10, 1943, on Hazelton Lane in the little village of Doaktown, New Brunswick (NB). I have been told that I got off to a pretty bad start. I was blessed to have so many caring and loving people around me the night I was born. Old Doctor Hamilton who apparently had arrived in a beautiful blue suit to deliver me became a little unravelled that night. Louise who I call Weezie can still remember the night I was born, and she isn't even that much older than me.

House where Perley was born.

Ruby Chute (Murphy) —"Nan" (left) & Zenith 'Granny' Ellison (right) — Great grandmother. b. 1877 d. 1961.

Back in the day, it seemed that everyone was one big family with neighbours helping neighbours and families helping families. So you see, it was magic, even back then, that I ended up with such a beautiful and caring person like Weezie and our Nan, Ruby Chute, and her husband who we called Uncle Nelson Chute. Nelson and Ruby Chute brought up my mom, Edith, and Louise Duncan (Weezie). Both girls were from different families, and people often looked after children whose parents had died or left them. Back in the day, if a family was poor or had a lot of children, and someone needed a boy to help on the farm or a girl to help in the kitchen, there was no paper work—just the exchange. So it was in Doaktown and that is how we ended up with a combined family, which my mom was grateful for as it made the heavy load a little lighter.

My Memory about Perley's Birth
by Louise 'Weezie' Duncan

It all began on a very cold night; it was 30 degrees below zero (Fahrenheit) and I remember there was a big full moon. I guess you could say the magic began seventy-three years ago on February 10, 1943, in a small village called Doaktown. In those days, there were no hospitals; the babies were born at home and the doctor came to the house with a midwife. Dr. Hamilton arrived in a nice blue suit with his horse and sleigh and Perley Edward Palmer was eventually born, weighing in at less than 2 pounds. Perley was what the doctor called a "blue baby."

Louise Duncan, Aldon Duncan, Don Duncan, Susan Duncan, Ruby Chute, Doug Duncan, Perley, and Linda Duncan - Christmas 1959

Weezie (Louise Duncan) and Perley.

There were no incubators back then and the doctor yelled for me to get two tubs of water, one hot tub and one cold tub, which I rushed to do, at his urgency. The doctor then began ducking the baby into the hot tub and then into the cold tub until all of a sudden we heard a small cry—that was when he was given the name of "Bubby." Then Bubby was silent and we prayed out loud that our Bubby would survive.

The doctor told Mom to wrap him in a warm blanket and put "it" on the oven door, and if "it" was living in the morning, dress "it" and put a diaper on it." We sat up all night and kept a vigil going and many a prayer was said. Then a miracle happened, we heard a small cry and then Bubby had his first meal, which consisted of a mixture of one ounce of water and sugar. We also put Bubby on the window ledge in the daytime in a shoe box to let the sun warm him. Day by day, he got stronger. Our Bubby was going to make it!

Bubby's Mom was very ill and had a hard time recovering after Bubby was born. Times were tough back then, and Bubby's Mom worked hard to make ends meet. There wasn't much employment so Bubby's Dad enlisted in the army and was sent to Camp Borden and later to Germany. Bubby and his mom stayed on at our house for the winter. My dad enlisted in the army as did many other men, which left us women to fend for ourselves. Bubby and his mom moved back to their own home in the spring when his dad got home from the army.

Bubby grew into the wonderful loving man he is today. There are many stories in between.

Bubby and I have and always will be connected.

                        Love you, Bubby,
                        Weezie

My Earliest Memories in Doaktown

I do have a few memories of when we lived in Doaktown. One time, I was out in the field opposite the house and I cut my foot really bad. I ran into the house and right off the bat, my Nan ran for the iodine bottle. Every time I cut myself, she would get out that old iodine, which I never liked because it always hurt so badly. Well, she opened that bottle, and I took off running. She chased me about two hundred yards across that field, and she caught me. She bent that leg up and she poured the whole bottle on that cut— boy, did that smart! I hated that iodine bottle and what was in it, but looking back I can see that she did the right thing. Ivan and Roger were my younger brothers, and I also have a sister; none of us liked being treated with that iodine bottle, but we all survived. Seemed like my mom was always having a baby, and I was happy to help her any way I could, even when I was young. Not to mention the fact that I was smaller than most other boys my age, but I seemed to be very intuitive for some reason, which I have always considered a gift–well, for the most part. ☺

I also remember being outside in the field and I pooped myself. I did not know what kind of trouble I was going to get in, so when I went inside I said, "Mama, cow poop on Baba." I obviously was quite creative to come up with that one even back then. Nothing happened other than I got sprayed down with the hose and away I went again looking for another adventure.

There was a camp owned by a man named Tom Boyd at the top of Allison Hill. We didn't have a lot to do in Doaktown, but I remember how beautiful it was back there. It seemed magical to be on the property and just look in the windows at all the beautiful furniture and surplus of things in the room. The camp was about a mile back in the woods. Doaktown is world famous for its salmon fishing and there were many guides willing and able to help Americans find their prey. Leonard Bower, a childhood friend of mine, and I would trek back to that camp. We would go and look in the windows because it was full of stuffed animals. There were fish, bears, and other animals on the wall. The camp was so nice and the veranda was so well made. I heard that camp burned down years later. They were good times in Doaktown, because we had no TVs back then and we found lots to do outside.

In the fall of 1949, I started Grade 1 at the old Doaktown school. I only went for two weeks because we moved to Marysville, which is part of the hometown I still live in. I really liked the school and knew most of my classmates, only because Doaktown was not a big place. I was in for a big shock moving towards a big town. The new school was massive in my eyes. I missed my friends from Grade 1, but whatever my family did, we did it together. Funny thing, a few years ago in 2014, I got a call to go back to Doaktown School. I was asked if I would do a magic show for the students. It was pretty cool to be called to perform magic in the school where I started out so many years before.

We moved to Marysville when I was six. Dad went to work in the cotton mill, along with so many others back then. Actually, the community was built around the cotton mill, and the jobs it created. We lived in a brick house, which is still standing, owned by Norris and Birdie Palmer who were relatives of ours. They were so good to mom and us kids and, boy, did we have some good meals there. I was happy my mom had such great and caring support. I remember we stayed there while Dad was building our house on Gregory Avenue, which was not that far from the brick house and our relatives.

I can still see Dad building our house; he would dig the earth to make a hole and he had a horse and some kind of a scoop. He would dig the hole and the scoop would haul out a bucket full of earth and the horse would pull it away, and that is how the foundation was dug for that house. I was amazed at how it was done and watched as the foundation was built as much as I could. I remember they used huge rocks for the foundation, and it was quite something to see it come together.

Meanwhile, I had started Grade 1 at the Alexander Gibson Memorial School in Marysville. Our family was very poor back in those days. All I ever had to wear were second-hand clothes that someone gave us. I will never forget this guy, Herman Gregory, because he gave my mom a pair of britches for me. They stuck way out on the sides, but somehow mom cut them all down to size and put them on me. They were the worst looking things and I had to go to school with them on. I felt so ashamed: I was sure everyone was looking at those old britches. The kids at school all made fun of me because I had no clothes to wear–I was small. The first year in school I had no shoes so I had to go in my bare feet. Actually, maybe it made me a better person: I don't really know because it sure didn't feel that way at the time. We had some great school teachers in Marysville. I remember Fanny Young, my Grade 1 teacher, because she was patient and nice to us. While I stayed at the same school, our family ended up moving again.

My younger brother, Ivan, recalls that in 1950, we moved again to 43 Gregory Avenue, where we lived for about three years. Ivan seems to have a better memory than me about those days. I do remember I was always drawn towards going to church, even as a young boy. When the house was finished, Ivan remembers it was in 1950, that we all moved into Gregory Avenue–all six of us. Sadly, after all that work and moves for my mom, we only lived there for three years. There was one bright spot though and that was a friend we met. His name was George Dayton and guess what his nickname was–you guessed it, Bubby. He remembers well that we lived on Gregory Avenue in Marysville not far from his home, and I remember going to church with his family.

Bubby Dayton Recollections

I lived at the corner of Gregory Avenue and Canada Street. Perley and I were near the same age and were together in some early elementary grades at Alexander Gibson Memorial School. My dad and mom filled the positions of the Sunday school superintendent and secretary, respectively, at what was then the Argyle Street Pentecostal Church. My dad had a '48 Chev panel "truck" as a vehicle at that time and always used it to take a load of children to Sunday school. The vehicle had only two original single-person seats, but my dad installed an old car seat lengthways in the back, with the seat back against the driver's side. In the small space that was left next to the rear door, he placed a plank bench crossway. Perley and I were occupants of that plank bench next to the back door, along with two or three other small children. (I believe some of Perley's siblings were also passengers, but I have no definite recollection.)

Apparently there must have been some kind of rivalry between us because I clearly recall the efforts Perley and I made to antagonize each other on Sunday mornings as we sat on the truck bench looking out the back window. He would call me "Date square," a takeoff on my surname, "Dayton," and I would call him "Palm tree," obviously because his surname was "Palmer." This name calling would continue until the loser failed to retaliate. Perley and I were not only good friends when we were young; somehow we both share the same nickname, "Bubby" even to this day.

Your lifetime friend
Bubby [George] Dayton

1948 truck Perley and Bubby drove in.

Perley's Memories

In 1953, Ivan remembers we moved back closer to the cotton mill again. We moved to a place called the "Old Hotel." The old hotel is torn down now, but it was just down from the old post office in Marysville.

The hotel was pretty nasty but it had low rent. It used to be a hotel at one time, but now it was filled with poor families. I remember being happy to meet so many new friends and we all lived under the same roof. The problem was I still had no real good clothes to wear and I felt my poverty, especially when I went to school.

The problems in school began in Grade 4 when I ran up against my teacher, Ms. Manzer. I honestly believe that woman did not like kids because she gave me the strap almost every day. Buddy Chase–yes, his name was Buddy, also was kind of a little rascal, and I guess I must have been too, because we were always getting the strap from Ms. Manzer.

One day I made a terrible mistake. I went up and she gave me the strap like she always did. She strapped at me and, after I went back to my seat she glared at me and I just smiled back–that was a bad mistake. She made me go back up again and she said, "I'll wipe that smile off your face." Well, she turned the ruler on its edge and strapped me with it and, oh boy, that one really hurt. You know, by the end of Grade 4, it got so the strap didn't even hurt anymore.

The Palmer family—1953.

She was a very cruel lady and it affected my grades. I mean–how can you learn from someone like that? I found my escape by playing little league baseball, which I loved from the beginning. We had lots of fun outside school, and made our own good times. Mom made sure we went to church, Cubs, and other community groups that I loved being part of.

People That Impacted my Younger Life

There were a few people in my life that had a huge impact on me when I was young, and I did tell them how they made a difference in my life. One of them was Doug McCullum. He was my Sunday school teacher and the other was Gordon Simmons who was a minister at the church I went to. We all loved Doug because he really cared and he was such a special teacher; he taught us not to smoke, not to drink, not to swear, and all that stuff. I took his advice and never did those things throughout my life. Nate Merrill, my Cub master, was the salt of the earth. He was a great man and had a real influence on my life when I was young.

The one thing I loved was playing baseball. My long-time friend, Billy Hanson, sent me a picture as a reminder of all the great times we had playing baseball as kids and attending church, and going to groups. All of these extracurricular activities, along with caring teachers, and people, helped me get through those early school years in Marysville.

My mom and I were very closer. She was a very hard-working woman and was employed at the Metropolitan store on Queen Street. She was a good mom in every way and, boy, could my mom cook! She could even make chocolates! I remember they looked like the chocolates in the packages, and she would make ice-cream and things like that. One of my favourite things Mom made was a dessert called bread and goody. It was made with milk, bread, and sugar. We would stir it all up and it was delicious.

While we were poor, we would always manage to find some food to eat. Many nights I used to cook the supper for everyone, and when I saw Mom coming home when I looked out the window, after many long hours of work, I would hide the food. When she came in, we would chat and she would say, "What's for super tonight, Bubby?" and I would say, "Oh, nothing tonight, Mom. I didn't make supper tonight." She would say, "Oh, I smell something really good." Then I would bring the food out and we would have a great laugh; Mom was always so grateful. I have many loving and fond memories of Mom. She made me want to be a better person and she never demanded that I help out; she always gave me that choice, which is why I love her so much.

The Life and Times of Perley the Magician 21

Perley's little league team.
Picture by *The Daily Gleaner* on Baseball Hill 1958.

Picture of Marysville Youth
Seated on Bleachers of Baseball Hill

Back Row - from *Left to Right*

1	2	3	4	5	6	7	8	9	10	11
Paul MacPherson	Glendon (Cob) Boyce	Wayne (Hike) McPherson (ball hat)	Bobby Kenny	Buddy Chase	Ron (Thumper) Buchanan	Doug Harrison	Richard Collins (ball hat)	Kent MacPherson	Ken White	Millard Savage

Middle Row - from *Left to Right*

1	2	3	4	5	6	7	8	9	10	11
Lee Johnson (round brim hat)	Charlie Hickey (peak hat)	Perley Palmer (glasses)	Darrell Sturgeon		Paul Fallon	Neil Watt			Bunny Gorman -- or -- David Watts (ball hat & ice cream)	(Dunc) Johnson (up-turned brim hat)

Front Row - from *Left to Right*

1	2	3	4	5	6	7	8	9	10
Allen (Skippy) Stafford (box popcorn)	John (Brick) McCafferty Jr.	Wayne Mann	Billy Hanson (peak on side – food in hand)	Rick Chase	Frank Pieroway	Art Currie (pop bottle)	George Farrell	Terry MacDonald	Eddie Peterson (Kid squatting – cowboy hat & bag)

Seating chart submitted by Bill Saunders

There was another person that helped me develop my character and who I looked up to and that was my 'Nan' Ruby Chute. She was so kind to me. She loved to pray and loved God. Nan and Nelson Chute had moved to Marysville from Doaktown, like our family. They lived close to us and I used to go to her house a lot, just to get out of our house. Ruby smoked and even though she was United Pentecostal; she was just the salt of the earth to me.

She used to roll the tobacco in one of those old long cigarette machines and make a whole bunch of them at once. She would cry because she wanted to stop smoking so bad. She pounded into my head, "Bubby, whatever you do, don't ever start smoking because if you do–you probably won't be able to stop." I took her advice and that was good advice. I loved her so much; I knew it would break her heart if I ever smoked and so I never did. I never had one in my mouth to see what it would taste like. She smoked all those years and she tried everything known to man to quit, but she smoked right up until she died; my Nan, I loved her so much. I loved going to visit my Nan, because she was so kind and sweet. She put love in my heart that is still there.

Poverty kind of leaves that murky stamp on people, especially when you're young and unaware of how cruel some people can be. Thank God that somehow I could always see the light at the end of the tunnel. When the Sullivans moved into the neighborhood, it was a like a bonfire had started. The Sullivans lived over the post office. Well, there was quite a crop of those Sullivans. There was Bill, Brian, Barry, Bonnie, Teddy, Danny, and Leonard. I remember Mrs. Grace Sullivan would wash me up for church, and I would tag along with all of them. I think Mrs. Sullivan even gave me a bath before church a couple of times. I hung around with the Sullivan boys a lot.

A Few Stories by Barry Sullivan

Perley (lft.), Barry's wife Chip, Ivan and Barry (rt.)

Dear Perley,

Thanks so much for giving me the privilege of being part of your story. Our family moved from Front Row (River Street) in Marysville to 27 Mill Street in 1955, after the cotton mill shut down for a few years. We happened to live very close to what we called the Old Green Hotel. In fact, there was only one brick house between us and the hotel. This meant that we had lots of friends from the huge hotel, which was full of families who had moved there to be close to the cotton mill.

Most of the people in the town of Marysville worked there. One of those families was the Palmers who we took to immediately because they were so friendly and we had so much in common–we were all poor! One hot summer day, the Palmers, an enterprising bunch, decided to start their own circus in the area surrounding the Old Green Hotel, which had a huge garage with about ten spots the size of our one-car garages today! Each hotel resident had the privilege of using one.

The circus was small, but it gained the interest of all those who lived in the hotel and some other kids on Mill Street. Roger, Perley's younger brother, set up a shooting range where you could buy balls and throw them at bottles he had set up in the back of the garage. If you could knock down the bottles standing on one another, you would win a prize of some sort. I thought this should be a piece of cake so I gave Roger my money and aimed at the bottles thinking I was about to take home a nice prize. First ball I missed, second ball I missed, so I picked up the last ball and aimed at the bottles and I struck them dead on and nothing happened,

Barry Sullivan

the bottles never budged because the Palmers had nailed the bottles so they wouldn't fall. I chased Roger until I caught him and made him cough up the money I had invested in the Palmer enterprise.

One day Perley and my older brother, Lenny (Leonard), went fishing on the old dam just above the bridge that crosses the Nashwaak close to the old cotton mill. After fishing for a while and probably catching a few sunfish, Lenny hooked a huge sucker fish, which has a huge round-shaped mouth that gives them a grotesque looking face and is slimy as an eel. Perley, being a few years younger than Lenny took one look at that monster when Lenny pulled the sucker in: It landed right beside Perley. The last Lenny saw of Perley was his backside hightailing it down the railway tracks toward home. Lenny would tell this story to anyone who would listen for the rest of his life at Perley's expense and always get a hearty laugh from all who would listen. I don't believe Perley ever went fishing with my brother, Lenny, after that incident!

We never had a TV in our house until long after most of our friends' families had one. We would go door to door at night asking if we could come in and watch Gene Autry or Hop-Along Cassidy with them. The Palmers declared one day that they had a new coloured TV. We rushed over to the Green Hotel, up three flights of stairs to see this amazing rare coloured TV. There it was plunked right in the middle of their living room. Yes, sir, our first look at a coloured TV and, boy, we were excited. They turned it on and pulled a plastic red sheet down over the screen that was attached to the top of TV. What a disappointment that was, the first coloured TV was nothing, but an old TV with coloured plastic sheets attached to top of it. Yes, they were entrepreneurs and creative–and loved to see people laugh–even when they were young.

We always have a great chuckle about our childhood memories and all the fun we had. We might have been poor, but we had fun in those early years growing up in Marysville.

                          Love you, Perley.
                          Your friend,
                          Barry

Perley's Friends and Fun

Charlie Hickey was a real good friend and his folks had a restaurant in Marysville. We hung out together for years, and we did a lot of crazy things along the way. We used to go out on Halloween. Charlie recalls that we used to put on some kind of a skit. I don't remember, but we did have great times. I remember one night a few of us guys were at the restaurant and this truck pulled up. We happened to notice that the truck was full of barrels of apples, and there were no lids on them. Well, the boys conned me into getting up and throwing them down some apples. Like a dummy, I climbed up on top of the barrels. It took me a while to get up there and start tossing the apples down to the boys. I didn't notice the guy get back into his truck, and then the motor started and we took off. The only thing that saved me was that we were on a really steep hill, and the guy couldn't get the truck going too fast so I managed to jump off. I guess my heart will always be in Marysville because I have wonderful memories of the good old days. While I had those two special teachers, I always felt out of place in school. Outside of school, weekends were whole different stories with my pals.

Back Row (L-R): Roger, Owen, Barry,
Bill, Ivan and Perley's son Michael.
Front row: Perly and daughter Faye.

Charlie Hickey's Memories

There are so many memories that flood my mind when I think about Perley and the years we have spent together. Although, as many of you already know, once you meet Perley, you can never forget him. I am going to write about the memories that are vivid in my mind.

One day Perley and I were in our family restaurant and he choked on a large black jawbreaker. For those that don't remember them, we could buy three jawbreakers for a penny. Those candies were about the size of a marble and hard as a rock. Fortunately, my dad noticed that Perley was choking and turning an ashen colour. My dad quickly grabbed Perley and turned him upside down, while patting him on the back. To everyone's relief, especially Perley's, out flew the jawbreaker.

Summer was always a great time for us in Marysville. We played "kick the can" almost every night. This was a huge favourite. Perley and I would get all the kids in the neighbourhood to join in. Another summer event was climbing on the CNR boxcars sitting on the railway near the post office. We knew the CNR men were tired from a long day and that they were resting, but that just made us more eager to bug them. We didn't mean anything by it; we were kids and just wanted some fun. Boy, did we move when those guys got irritated enough to chase us away. It was scary and great fun, but then, again, Perley and I always outran them as they were too tired and always gave up. We kept right on doing it though, even with the risk of them catching us. I think we liked the thrill of it. We needed these good times to balance out homework and school, and to prepare us for our unknown future.

Perley and School

Meanwhile back at school in Marysville, one of my favourite teachers was in Grade 6–the late Clyde Ferrell. He was from a small town called Minto. What a wonderful teacher he was: I did well in his class, because he made learning interesting and fun. He was such a kind person and he really cared about his students. I tried so hard to do well for him because he was so nice. It just goes to show you that when someone is nice, you try so much harder. When someone is hateful, you really don't try. It was a good lesson of how I wanted to treat people in my life. I remember years later, I was asked to do some shows in Minto, where Clyde Ferrell was from. Clyde came to see me, and he told me how proud he was of me and how I turned out. I feel fond memories of school when I think of him.

One of the places I never felt a lot of kindness was at our school dances. I felt like a wallflower when I used to go to the dances. I was so insecure and I had no nice clothes to wear. I would go to the dances but always stand back out of the way. I was scared to death to ask a girl to dance because I knew for sure she would say, "No." I remember when they had the girls pick a guy to dance. I hated that, too, because none of the girls ever asked me to dance. When the girls picked a guy to dance in the Paul Jones dance, I would try and stand up closer to the front, but was never asked to dance. My clothes were so shabby that I didn't feel any girl would want to hang out with me anyway.

Everything erupted in 1958, and our whole family split up. It was during this time that our parents divorced, with each parent going their separate way and eventually re-marrying. Mom moved to Ontario and took Ivan. Weezie recalls that Roger and I stayed with her and our Nan and Uncle Nelson Chute. I guess that is how I ended up at Albert Street School, and had one of the best teachers ever.

In Grade 7, my last year of school, I had another wonderful teacher, Al Kingston. Al Kingston taught at Albert Street School and was a kind man, too. I never felt that I was a very good student. I didn't seem to get my lessons done the way they ought to have been done. Mr. Kingston had a lot of patience with me. I think he took a shine to me. I learned from him, but that was to be my last year in school. I had to go to work because our family needed money. Years later, I did a magic show and Al Kingston was the MC. He spoke so highly of me as he introduced me, and kind of bragged me up. Because I didn't do great in school, that was a very proud moment for me.

Tribute From Allison Kingston

Perley was a student in my Grade 7 class at Albert Street School. The uncertainties in his family left him with little choice, but to leave school as a teenager and become self-supporting. Those uncertainties undoubtedly affected his ability to function effectively in a school setting. His friendly personality and previously hidden talents shone when he dedicated himself to becoming a magician. His unique ability and commitment to entertainment have given many of all ages, including me, a moment of wonder and escape from the routines of daily living. Whenever and wherever we met through the years since those Albert Street days, there was always a moment for a bit of "Perley Magic." Though I was his teacher for a short time, I have appreciated his friendship for many years. I take no credit for the development of his remarkable talent for entertainment. We have joked some time that his first act of magic was his vanishing from my classroom. It is a pleasure to offer a tribute to a former student who has become a remarkable entertainer.

                          Your teacher and friend
                          Allison Kingston

Life Moved On

After I quit school in Grade 7, I got an apartment out of town. It was no bigger than a clothes closet, with a little couch to sleep on and a hot plate to cook on. I had to find somewhere to go on my own after my parents split up. Mom moved to Toronto and Dad moved to Tracadie with a woman. I was left to survive on my own. It was a very difficult time for our entire family. Mom had made me a responsible young man by this time, and I knew how to survive.

The room did not work out all that great and, thankfully, I was able to move back in with Nan. I started babysitting for Terry Jardine and his wife, as a result of an ad I followed up on. They lived in the Wilmot Apartments. I loved babysitting and making the children laugh. The only problem was I needed way more money than that to live on.

One night when Terry was paying me, I asked him "Where can I get a good job? To my surprise, he told me to come to Sobeys on Monday morning wearing a white shirt and a black bow tie. Well, it took me by surprise, and I said, "I don't know anybody down there." Terry had had a few beers and he kind of slurred and said, "Yes, you do. I am the manager and I just hired you." I was so excited. Over the weekend, I scraped up the shirt and a black bow tie. I showed up for work early on Monday morning. The first thing Terry said in that gruff voice of his was, "What are you doing here?" I explained to him that he had hired me and asked him if he remembered. He just grunted and told me to start packing groceries.

There I was working at Sobeys and I was so proud. I don't know how many times I carried out groceries and the car trunks would fall on my head because I was so short. I have many good memories of working at Sobeys. Terry was a great boss. Outside work, I loved to play pool to try and scrape up a little extra money here and there. I loved old cars and still liked having fun.

I happened to get a call from one of my oldest friends recently and asked if he had any recollection of our teens, which I knew he would, and asked if he would send along something for the book. Larry was so happy to be asked and he sent the following message:

Memories From Larry Ackerson

I met Perley in 1958 and, at the time, he was babysitting for a minimal wage for Terry Jardine who was the manager of Sobeys on Queen Street where I worked. Perley told me the story about how he managed to acquire a job at Sobeys. When Perley told me the story and you know how mesmerizing only Perley can be, we became instant best friends. We worked together at Sobeys for three years and had lots of laughs at work and many a good time after work because we both loved adventures.

Larry Ackerson

On one occasion, we were on a double date: I had a 1954 Oldsmobile that Perley really loved. When the evening was over, I drove to Don and Monica McNally's apartment, where I was living at the time. When we arrived, I turned to Perley and asked him to pick me up the next morning. He looked at me with eyes big as saucers and said, "I don't have a driver's licence." I said, "That's okay." Perley proceeded on with a huge smile.

Perley riding along

One weekend, Perley, Dave Peterson, Ray Soucie, and I drove to Boston. On the way back, I had a bad muffler and it was loud. The police pulled me over and, of course, fined me. Between the four of us, we didn't have enough money to cover the fine, so we were held until the fine was paid. Thanks to Terry Jardine, money arrived and we finally returned home. Maybe Perley's magic was working back then? Who knows, but we shared many more wonderful times together.

In 1961, I was transferred to Moncton and, in 1962, I left for Toronto, returning to Fredericton in 1968 where I bought a catering business. Perley and I only saw each other occasionally as we were both busy with our individual lives by then.

Over the last four years, we have become very good friends again. I enjoy playing pool with him at Frank's Finer Diner four to five times a week. In the beginning, he would beat me twenty out of twenty. However, this year, we played twenty games and I was able to win ten! I just had to throw that in, because everyone knows Perley is the Champ at pool.

Although I spend my winters in Florida, I try and call him every week. I have known Perley for fifty-nine years and consider him one of my best friends.

                        Sincerely,
                        Larry

Perley's Journey

For some reason, I love being around people. I am overwhelmed by the connections I have made during my life and still do. We are putting a lifetime into a few pages, and hope that the pictures will add to the enjoyment of your time reading the book and, as you come along on the journey of my life. I appreciate each person who is helping and those of you who are reading my story. Sounds to me from Larry, Charlie, Owen, and Dougie Duncan that when I was sixteen, my life really took off in a new direction.

Another Vivid Memory From Charlie Hickey

I remember when Perley was around sixteen; he bought an old Cadillac convertible. He had a little crush on a cousin of mine who lived in Jacquet River. We made all the arrangements, and Perley and I started out on a Friday just after supper to go there. We were driving along, somewhere between Newcastle and Bathurst. Back in the day, the road wasn't that great and the trip took more time. Around midnight, we heard, "boom." You guessed it–we had a flat tire. We were in the middle of nowhere and it was close to midnight. We decided the best thing to do was to stay put till morning. We went to sleep until daybreak and then headed out to knock on a farmer's door. Back in the day, people were very helpful and trusting, and, of course, with Perley's big smile, how could he not help. He transported us, along with the tire to the nearest garage, which was about ten miles away. We finally got the tire fixed and were on the road again. Perley got to meet my cousin on Saturday afternoon. This was quite an adventure, and then we turned around and came back to town the next day. Perley and I go way back. I have the fondest memories of our childhood and am so proud to call him my friend.

      Your old pal,
      Charley Hickey

My Teens and New Adventures

When I was sixteen years old, I came across a little pool room, which was just around the corner from Sobeys. I became fascinated with Roy's Poolroom. Because I was sixteen at the time, I wasn't allowed in because, back then, you had to be eighteen to get in the pool hall. So I found a way to get in there on Mondays, which was my day off. I would go in and help cleanup, clean the tables off, and when I was done, old Roy and I would shoot some pool. I think he got me to help clean because he was a heavy man and he couldn't lean over. Roy was a great pool player and he and I began to shoot pool for a couple of hours. There would be no one around in the morning so we had a great time and I learned a lot about pool from old Roy. There wasn't much police presence around Roy's and I really shouldn't have been in there, but I am glad he let me in the door.

 I have one vivid memory about playing pool at Roy's. I was about seventeen years old at the time. I was sitting on the steps of the pool hall when this man walks by. I knew he was from out of town because I had never seen him before. Back then, everyone pretty well knew everyone. Anyway, the man looked at me and said, "Do you want to shoot some pool, young fella?" I looked up at him and said, "Well, I guess I could." Well, we used to shoot for five or ten cents, which was quite a lot of money. This man informed me that we would be shooting for $2 a game. I said, "How much?" The guy replied, "$2." That was unheard of back then. I remember it was around 5 p.m. I said, "OK" because I had $5 in my pocket and thought that was all I could lose. The guy proceeded to open this beautiful case, which was all velvet inside, and then he removed an amazing pool cue. I thought that I was in big trouble, but acted confident anyway. I always loved a challenge and tried to do my best, regardless of the circumstances. We played pool for seven hours, and for $2 a game. Around 12 a.m., old Roy hollered down and said, "Make that your last game. I am closing up." I had money in every pocket, and the guy said to me, "You have over $100 of my money in your pocket. This cue is worth over $100, and if you win this game, I will give you the cue and the case; if I win this game, you empty your pockets." We both agreed and he had the first break, and I said, "break 'em up." He hit those balls and I swear I thought he was going to split them in half because he hit them so hard." Those balls went around that table and not one dropped, but they spread so good for me, that I told the guy he could put the cue back in the case. I was a good shot from all the practicing I had done and I ran that board and never missed a shot. He fired the cue and the case on the table and walked out. He never said a word and I never saw that man again. I went home with $112 in my pocket, which was about a month and half pay back then, and I had the beautiful case and cue; that was a lot of money. I felt like I had won the lottery. What a night to remember!

I got away from pool for many years, and I just got back into it about ten years ago. I play a lot of pool today and enjoy the game and the friends I know and meet. I don't care if I win money today, but back then I needed the cash. Sobeys was my main source of income, and I still have so many good memories from those days. Weezie recalls that I was quite the Casanova in those days. She remembers I always drove a big fancy sporty car and had a great hairdo. Can you imagine that? However, I always tried to smile and be happy at my job, just like my mom always was after a long shift. My attitude attracted some wonderful friends and people.

Perley, Carole, Harley Sabre, (front) Mr. Terry Jardine.

I remember this one woman that would come to the store—boy, was she dressed to kill! She drove a big Cadillac and it was obvious that she had money. She didn't have a man and she would drive herself up here from Florida to be here in the summer. I carried her groceries all summer and we got to know each other pretty good. She was a lovely lady and always gave a small tip when I carried out her groceries. At the end of the summer, she asked me if I would be interested in driving her back to Florida and she would fly me back home. I was only in my teens; I declined because I was afraid and I didn't feel comfortable about doing that. She got someone from the store to drive her, and that was fine. In the grocery business, I met a lot of wonderful people. I must have liked it a little bit because I spent over fifty years working in grocery stores.

My most vivid memory of working happened on a Friday night. It was a really busy night, and people were going everywhere in the store. My job was carryout boy. I had a little smock with Carryout Boy written on it. Every checkout had someone bagging groceries, and when the customer was ready to go, the packer would call out, "Cart please." There were three carryout guys and whoever was closest would get the groceries and carry them out to the cars. I heard someone call for a carryout and I was the closest. I ran over and grabbed the groceries. It was heavy because there was a case of carnation milk and another big box.

I started following the lady and she went across the street. I said, "Lady, the parking lot is over here." The lady turned around and said, "I just live up the street." I hoped it was not far because my arms were killing me. I had no idea how far we were supposed to walk with groceries so I kept following her up the street. After about two blocks, I asked her, "Lady where do you live?" She turned and said, "I just live up there a bit." By now, I felt like my arms were breaking and she was clipping right along. Every once in a while, she would turn around and say, "Boy, you fellows take the groceries a long way." I explained that I didn't think we were supposed to come this far. Finally, we arrived at her place and, as I followed her, she began to slam the door on me. I frantically said, "Lady, don't you want your groceries?" She turned around and said, "They are not my groceries. I thought you were out on a delivery."

I thought that I was going to be in real trouble when I got back. After all, it took about half an hour to follow that lady. I started back and I met Don Donovan about a block away, and I just asked if he would please take the groceries, because I couldn't carry them anymore. Don was my co-worker and he said, "When you get back, Jardine is waiting to fire you." I was ready. The poor lady who had actually bought the groceries was still at the store waiting for them. I knew I was in trouble, but it was an honest mistake. I worked the rest of my shift. Mr. Jardine never fired me, and I learned another good lesson that night.

Sobeys did have a bowling team and I loved that. Harley Clark and Don McNally bowled on that team. I remember Lawson Motors had a team; we were bowling this night, and this big guy threw the ball and they all went down, but one. He hollered, "Fall, you fool!" but the pin didn't drop. We always had a great time. But there was one time, I did fall.

Everyone at Sobeys knew there was this guy was shoplifting. So this one day, I told Mr. Jardine and Terry Burns, another manager, that I could catch him. I went up on top of the celling, which had small holes in the tile, because I was the smallest and followed the guy . . . well, guess what! The roof caved in and I landed right on top of the culprit! We always got things done at Sobeys, one way or another.

We started up a little ball team at Sobeys, and we would play around at various places and some pick-up teams–nothing serious. Harley was the pitcher and I was the catcher. We had a lot of fun and met a lot of people. Eventually, while I was still working at Sobeys, I took up playing ball in a more serious way and I eventually became a pitcher. Some noon hours, my good friend, Jerry McGilligan, would come over and we would go up to the top floor of Sobeys and play catch for 45 minutes. We threw that ball so hard; it was great practice.

I remember other things about Sobeys. I was young and really didn't know much about the birds and the bees, and definitely did not know what a homosexual or a pedophile was. I remember they hired this little man as a custodian, and I thought he was kind of strange. The first week he started work, he began to buy me treats, like candy and chocolate bars. On Thursday morning, he said, how would you like to go to the drive-in tomorrow night? I said in an excited and kind of louder voice, "The drive-in; boy, would I ever!" That afternoon I was working when Mr. Jardine came down the aisle: I said, "Boy, Mr. Jardine, that new man you hired is some nice." He looked at me and said, "What do you mean, Bobby?" I excitedly told him that the new guy had been buying me candy all week and Friday night he was going to take me to the drive-in. Mr. Jardine's face turned white and he said, "Where is he?" I wasn't sure where the guy was, but Mr. Jardine headed for the back door with his head down. I knew there was going to be trouble because when Mr. Jardine got mad, he always put his head down. I followed him to see what was going on. Well, he saw the new guy by the back door, grabbed him by the seat of his pants, and threw him right out the door. He told the guy,

"Never come back." Then he swung around to me and said, "Bobby, come with me to the office; we need to have a talk." Mr. Jardine always called me Bobby and that was fine with me. He straightened me out about a lot of things and especially the birds and the bees. Thinking back, Mr. Jardine was something like a dad because he was always looking out for my best interest.

I remember when I worked for Sobeys, Mr. Jardine used to take $1 a week out of my pay for two or three years and put it in the safe. When Allan Sherwood came to work at Sobeys, he had a 1953 Pontiac–actually when he came, he had a 1947 Plymouth, but he bought this 1953 Pontiac. He had it for about a year, when someone ran into the back fender and put a dent in it. Allan said to me, "Do you want to buy that car. I will sell it to you for $375?" That dent in the back fender didn't bother me any, so I went to Mr. Jardine and told him I wanted the money he had been saving for me because I wanted to buy Alan's car. Mr. Jardine said, "No, Bobby; I am not giving you that money." So on Tuesday, I went back to him and said, "Please, Mr. Jardine, can I have my money?" Once again he said, "No, Bobby." So Wednesday, I went back and asked again, "Please, Mr. Jardine, can I have my money?" Once again, he told me I was not getting that money. I went back again on Thursday and got the same response. On Friday, I went back and practically begged him for the money, and he finally gave it to me. Mr. Jardine was so mad and he told me he was never going to save any more money for me. I had an awful job getting the money out of him. It was my own money, but he wouldn't give it to me. I laugh about it now, but back then it wasn't funny because I wanted that car so bad. It was a good car and I think I kept it three or four years. I loved cars, pool, and baseball by now.

Tribute by Alan Lyons

Perley and I worked together at Sobey's grocery store when I was eighteen years old. He was the grocery manager and he took me under his wing and taught me a lot.

Perley offered to drive me to work as I had no vehicle; he showed up on his motorcycle. I quickly realized that he had no fear of driving. The road was packed with vehicles, but Perley barrelled through the oncoming traffic; I never said a word. The last thing I wanted was for him to think that I was afraid. Fall arrived and the days got cooler. Perley put his bike away and started to drive his car. His cars were always older and the tires held air so there was no need to change them.

Perley never saw a need to slow down; it was always 60 m.p.h.–no matter what the conditions. One day we started out; it was slushy and slippery. Traffic was moving slower so we passed several vehicles, then he pulled out into the passing lane and cut the wheels to move back into our lane, but nothing happened. The car skidded down the road and would not turn. There was an oncoming car getting closer and, all of a sudden, Perley's car cut across the road and stopped against a tree. We backed off the tree and continued on our way. Needless to say, it was always an adventure working with Perley.

Working in a grocery store required some evening work. On Thursdays, my shift started at 1 p.m. I came into work one Thursday and Perley met me right at the entrance. I could see that he was upset and I asked him what was wrong. He said he was in a real fix. There was an old man the washroom and that he had been there for two or three hours. He said, "I think he must be dead, but I'm a little leery of forcing the door open or looking over the top." He said, "Would you mind having a look?" Being young and always trying to impress. I said, Sure, I will." Well we went to the door of the washroom stall and it was obvious that someone was in there. You could see boots and trousers underneath the door. I spoke up loudly trying to get a response from the person inside–no answer. Perley said, "If I get a chair, will you climb up and look over top to see if the person is ok?" Reluctantly, I said I would. He got the chair and I hesitantly peeked over the top of the door and saw only a pair of boots and trousers. Perley busted a gut over that one.

Perley introduced me to my wife, Darlene, and eventually became the best man at our wedding, but not before he taught me a few things about life. Darlene and I went on our first date to the mall Christmas party at the Monsignor Boyd Center around the corner from my apartment. As usual, I would drink enough that I would feel at ease on the first date. Darlene and I had a great time, but, of course, the drinking got the best of me and I started to feel ill. She knew my apartment was close by and even though she had never been there, she suggested that she help get me to my room. My place wasn't much; a very small kitchen at one end and a single bed in one corner. The bathroom was down the hall and was shared with two other men. By the time, we reached my place, I was in no condition to do anything, but flake out on the bed passed out.

Darlene took a blanket and laid on the floor. Sometime in the night, I became aware of someone coming through my apartment door. It was Perley. I can still picture him sitting at my tiny kitchen table shaking his head back and forth, and looking at Darlene lying on the floor. Perley said, "Alan, Alan, Alan; I'm so disappointed in you. I really thought I'd taught you better than this." My life changed from that night on and all because of Perley. He is the best friend, boss, and mentor I ever had. Perley, you're one of a kind! Thanks for being my friend.

                          Love,
                          Alan

A Tribute and a Memory by Doug Duncan—Weezie's son

When I remember growing up and spending time at Nan and Gramps (Ruby and Nelson Chute), "Bubby" was like a big brother to us kids. He was always a sharp dresser who loved his car and his hair. Bubby loved sports, especially ball. He was the pitcher and always needed a catcher to practice- guess who the catcher was! Being ten years his junior, I was terrified and amazed at how hard and fast he could throw that ball, so it was with tattered glove and eyes shut I would hope and pray he would always hit the glove and he did!! I remember the time he lead us through the woods to show us a camp he built. It was the hottest day of the summer and the bugs would carry you away. When we finally got there, it sure wasn't much of a camp, but Bubby was some proud of it. Bubby always sees the glass half full, no matter what!

       Love 'ya, Uncle,
       Doug

Perley and Doug.

Life Moved Forward

I got married when I was twenty years old to Evelyn; a girl who worked at Sobeys. When I look back on those years, I realize I didn't know how to be the very best husband, and I was travelling around a lot; playing ball and going to ball games and things like that. We did have three beautiful children, who I was a good dad to. I guess I never really knew how to be a good husband back then–like I am today. I guess I was never close to my own Dad and he was not much of a role model when I reflect on my childhood. Actually he was a very rough man.

My dad and I were never close. I think towards the end of his life, Dad tried to get closer to me, but I never felt close to him even then. I used to go up to the Brookside Mall and sell clocks that I used to make. My dad used to come up to the mall and sit beside my display. I guess that was his way of showing he was proud of me. He would just sit there, sometimes for two hours, but he wouldn't say much.

My dad had emphysema and he would go in and out of the hospital a lot, and it got so we didn't think too much about it when he was admitted. I remember I was working at Tingleys one day and Phil McFarlane called me–that was Dad's doctor. Phil and I went to school together and knew each other quite well. Phil said, "You better get to the hospital right away if you want to see your dad alive, because he is really bad."

I got off the phone and called my brother, Roger. We landed at the hospital right about the same time. Dad had died five minutes before we got there, and I will never forget the look on his face. It was a look of sheer terror, like he was scared to death. I guess when you can't get your breath, it must be a horrible scary thing, and that is how he died. Funny, I did not feel any huge loss when Dad died, but I vowed again that I would never smoke, and I also had a deep desire to be a good dad and husband.

In 1968, a chap by the name of Lawrence Swazey came into the store and asked me if I would go to work for him. They were opening a big Kmart-Dominion Store. He offered me $65 a week and said they were unionized. I was making $45 a week as produce manger, but back then, I really needed the money. Times were tough in those days and I had three children and my wife to take care of so I jumped at the opportunity. I guess I should have talked it over with Mr. Jardine, because I hated that job from the first day I started. We were all so busy and the store was constantly full of people. The employees seemed to be separate from management because they were unionised. You could feel the tension and division. It seemed like the employees were the enemy. I just never liked working at the Dominion store.

One thing that I did like was playing baseball. After I moved to the Dominion, one of the guys, Melvin Spires, had a little industrial ball team at the store. He never had a pitcher on the team. I had been practicing pitching all summer, and told him I thought I could pitch. Later I moved up to a major softball league because somehow my pitching got good enough to land me pitching in a competitive league.

Melvin was so mad at me that he went to Mr. Swazey who was my boss at Dominion and tried to get me fired. He told Mr. Swazey, "You have to fire Perley." Mr. Swazey said, "Why?" Melvin explained that I wouldn't play ball for him and Mr. Swazey just said, "What has that got to do with Perley's job? Melvin tried hard to get me fired, but, of course, Mr. Swazey wouldn't so that was the end of that.

I started playing ball for different teams. I think the first team I played for was Marysville. I believe Butch Bailey was the manager. I was throwing pretty fast by then, so I was told. I eventually worked my way up pitching into the senior ball league. I played for General Dairies, Acadian Marble, and a number of other teams. I played hockey, ping pong, and tennis along with a number of other sports. I was pretty small, but I was told I could pitch fast. For some reason, pitching became one of my passions. Even then I liked working with my hands; I loved the game of baseball and my teammates. I met a lot of people playing baseball over the years.

I guess in was around 1974 that one of the supervisors from Sobeys happened to be in the store and he stopped to talk with me. He said, "Didn't you used to work for us?" He went on to say he that he would like to talk to me after work and to come over to the store. That man was Johnny Thornton. When I met with him, he offered me a job and gave me a raise and a promotion. I started back at Sobeys and I felt right at home again. I was used to making changes in my life.

In 1977, I got another visitor. Richard Tingley, the owner of Tingley's Grocery Store, came to visit me. He offered me a job in their new store, but I had just gotten five weeks' vacation built up. I explained that to Richard, and he said, "If you will come to work for me. I will pay you more and start you off with five weeks' vacation." Richard was such a good man, and the store was such a nice place to work that Owen Brewer and I would go in an hour early. We couldn't wait to get to work because we loved working for Richard Tingley. He still is a super nice friend and a wonderful person, and we go to breakfast once in a while. In fact, he gave me a lot of pictures for this book the last time we met. I worked for Tingleys for about twenty-five years, and loved every day there.

Tribute by Richard Tingley

Our people make the difference! This was the slogan for Tingley's Save Easy. Perley Palmer certainly personified this slogan during his long-term employment with us. I have always felt that our success in the retail grocery business was due to my good fortune in employing many wonderful people who helped create a "special" atmosphere in our supermarkets that once was described by one of our patrons as "a cocktail party without the liquor." Perley's character, personality, humour, along with his positive approach to life was infectious. Perley helped create an environment that was enjoyed by his co-workers and our customers.

Perley is very fond of children, and he would delight in guiding many of them to the bakery department where he would grab a fresh cookie for them. Of course, when he developed his magical talents, the children would enjoy magic, as well as their cookies. I was told that some of our customers changed their shopping habits to several visits as opposed to perhaps a weekly visit for the groceries, giving in to pressures from their children.

Perley was a talented fastball pitcher and he distinguished himself in city leagues for several years. He won a few MVP awards for our store team that competed each year with other Save Easy stores from around the province. He was an excellent pitcher and was able to throw a curve that resulted in numerous strikeouts and plenty of wins for our team.

Our Ball Team

Perley was a very dedicated employee and he took a great deal of pride in any of the awards or recognition that came our way. Perley told me that the national gold awards as "Independent Grocer of the Year" were a highlight for him, and his excitement for this achievement was obvious when the awards were brought home from Toronto and displayed on the store's wall.

Throughout his employment, Perley was always a willing participant in building any special displays, which were often competition winners. He was especially proud of his carpentry in the construction of the potato house that was part of a promotion for NB potatoes, where a trip to the Barbados was offered as a prize for the lucky winner.

Owen and Perley

Of course, there were several occasions when we were able to use Perley's magical skills to entertain. For several years, we had a special fundraiser day for "Characters Incorporated," a young singing and dancing group at the Nashwaaksis store. Perley's magic show was always popular at this event and enjoyed by young and old.

Perley is indeed a very special person: Tingleys was very fortunate to have him as an employee. He has gained tremendous respect from a wide circle of friends. His friend, Owen Brewer, would often say, "Is there anywhere that we could travel where you would not be recognized, Perley?" Many people have gained admiration and respect for the way Perley has handled adversity as it relates to the health issues he has faced in recent times. His upbeat and very positive outlook continues to keep him strong. How "special" is Perley? . . . not many people have a day named for them in their home town.

                       Your long-time friend,
                       Richard Tingley

Perley and Owen, with Darrell Spencer

When Tingleys had one store, the late Darrell Spencer worked there as the meat manager for Richard Tingley. When Richard opened a second store in Nashwaaksis, Darrell went over there as the store manager. Darrell did a wonderful job and he was more like a friend than a boss. I worked for Tingleys for over twenty-five years. I couldn't even begin to describe how much I enjoyed working for Tingleys. Being treated with appreciation and respect helps a person go a long way; that is just how I was treated when I worked for Tingleys.

Becoming a Magician

I was working at Tingleys when I really got interested in magic. I loved magic. There was this magician from England who would come on TV. I would stay up until midnight if I found out he was going to do a magic show. Magic intrigued me to no end at this point.

There was a furniture store next to Tingleys and the owner used to do this trick with a quarter. I was always asking him to show me this trick. When the store closed down, I went and pretty well begged the owner to show me that trick and he did. I used to love that trick and the children loved that trick, but that was the only trick I knew. One thing people would say, "Is that the only trick you know, Perl?" I would answer, "Yes, that is the only trick I know." I really wanted to find out how to do more tricks for the children.

Well, I decided to go all out as I was so fascinated by the smiles and laughter magic brought to people. I wanted to know more about how to perform.

What is a Magician?

The following describes a magician and what we do ("What Does a Magician do?," n.d.):

"A magician is someone who will entertain an audience by performing magic tricks, effects, or illusions. These tricks and illusions seem impossible or supernatural to the audience. The magician learns these magic tricks by practicing them over and over again, sometimes taking hundreds of hours to perfect. Sleight of hand tricks, especially require extensive practice, to ensure that the trick is executed without flaw while performing. A magician can find work by performing at restaurants, birthday parties, special events, and weddings, and, if especially charismatic and skilled, can also work their way up to performing in larger venues, including major night clubs, Las Vegas venues, and even make television appearances."

What Does a Magician do?

Audiences are in general very skeptical, and they watch intently so as to spot 'the trick.' A magician's techniques, however, have been perfected over time by constant practice and performance in order to withstand even the highest scrutiny. A magician will use visual, sensory, and auditory illusions in their tricks, because it is a well-known fact that a person's perception can contradict what is physically happening. Cognitive illusions are also used; by manipulating people's memory, their logic, and by misdirecting their attention (such as releasing a dove).

What Does a Magician do? (n.d.).

Perley Pursues Magic

I had heard about a magic shop in Toronto. I wrote them, sending $10 and received a catalogue with a lot of magic tricks. I spent about a month going through the catalogue, writing down the tricks I wanted to purchase. I called in my order and it came to around $1,900. When I hung up the phone, I thought to myself, what have I just done? The package arrived and wow, did I get a lot of tricks! The phone began to ring and it hasn't stopped since. Birthdays are still one of my favourite magic parties. My good friend, Owen, would help me figure out many of my new tricks and, through the years, we have had a wonderful time. I always loved magic and even before I started doing the real magic, I always had a few cards in my pocket to do a little card trick. That is how it all began. My buddy, Owen Brewer, helped me through the years, not just with magic, but with me becoming a better person and believing in myself.

Some of the Things I Remember About my Best Friend, Perley Palmer

Written by Owen Brewer

Owen Brewer

I've known Perley for more than forty years. We worked together at Tingley's Save Easy over twenty years in the produce department. Perley was a lot of fun to work with–if you could keep him working, because you see Perley liked to socialize and spend a lot of time in the snack bar drinking coffee with friends and laughing.

On any day, you could find five or six guys from the store out on the ball field behind the store playing American or screen ball. Oh, to be young again. This is bringing back so many great memories.

Perley and I used to love to build large displays in the produce department for the various contests our store held. Some of our displays were made of potatoes, strawberries, and apples and various other produce. We had so much fun putting the displays together.

Then we would get Darrell Spencer, our manager, to take pictures of the work we had accomplished. Low and behold, Perley and I won our fair share of first places, but we enjoyed doing the displays. It wasn't even work to us. It was always fun to go to work because we never knew what was going to happen on any day. I remember when Perley started to dabble in magic. He would buy the tricks, and we would set out in the staff room and try and figure them out.

Perley was so "sleight of hand," it was actually magical. He could find a way to do the tricks, and we were all amazed. Darrell Spencer was always the first person Perley would try his tricks out on. I mean if the manager was impressed, we knew that our customers would be, too.

Perley's magic has grown beyond anything either of us could believe. The more tricks Perley got, the better he got, and the more tricks he learned. Perley was excellent at lighting up the eyes of little children and even adults were left wondering how Perley did the magic. Perley had found his calling in life–to make people feel happy and smile. I am very proud of my friend, and to be part of this magic. It is kinda heartwarming that when Perley buys a new trick, he still brings it to me so we can figure it out together.

Back in the day, we would go to Boston or Montreal to a ball game. We would be sure to visit Hank Lee's magic store or other magic shops to stock up. Everyone had fun when Perley was around. I remember when we went to the ball games, we would get tickets way up in the nose bleed sections where you could hardly see the games. Then, all of a sudden, Perley would disappear, and about half an hour later, we would see him setting next to the dugout or in the front row! Perley would explain that all he did was a little magic trick and somehow he got someone's empty seat. Then Perley would turn and wave and laugh at us for sitting so far away; that was Perley–always magic! We always had so much fun after the games just touring around Montreal or Boston. With Perley, then and now, there is never a dull moment.

Perley always looked forward to organizing our ball tournaments. Perley was a pretty good pitcher and I was glad I was on his team. I was a pretty good batter, and that is where I always out hit him-ha ha! Back to the ball games; we would hit up the vendors of the store to sponsor us for pop and chips, water, and whatever else we could get our hands for prizes. We had great awards from Ben's Trophies for MVP and other winners. We were always a great team–still are best of friends throughout all the changes in our lives, careers, and Perley's magic.

Love ya,
Owen

Perley's Family Life and the Changes

As I mentioned, I did get married and we had three beautiful children. However, when your wife leaves you for somebody else–well, I felt very insecure after that happened. I started to wonder why anybody else would want me and that is how I felt. I didn't date anybody because I didn't have the nerve to ask anybody. I was sure they would say, "No." I didn't want to be hurt anymore so I never went on any dates for two or three years. I was very lonely during that period, and no matter how old you are, I know that people get lonely by themselves. It was a dark time in my life. I was one to believe that things would turn out and never to give up.

A friend of mine, Tony Buyting, had been after me to go to Parents Without Partners. I skipped out on him two weeks in a row, and I finally went because I knew he was never going to leave me alone. There were about twenty-five people there and they had different tables for groups to sit at. There were some ladies there and I thought they were quite old, and then I looked across the room. There was a lady about thirty-five years old; I thought she was really pretty and someone I would like to talk to. I asked Tony if he could get me moved to her table and he did. We started talking just small talk and I told her I worked at Tingleys. She told me she had a good friend that worked there by the name of Shirley McKinley. So the next day, I went to work and went to see Shirley and told her I had met a friend of hers. When I told her it was Valerie Ross, she said, "Don't you bother her, Perley! The last thing she needs is a man." I was kind of surprised and stepped back saying, "OK." Actually, I backed right off and I never called Valerie like I had planned, but she was on my mind. I was slowly becoming Perley the Magician when I met Valerie–way back then.

Perley and Valerie Meet: Our First Meeting—by Valerie Palmer

Valerie Palmer

In the fall of 1980, I met Perley at a Parents Without Partners meeting. Perley always said it was love at first sight. I was never comfortable in crowds and it helped to be seated next to this very friendly and outgoing man. The first thing I noticed was that Perley had the prettiest blue eyes and, throughout the evening, he kept me in stitches. After that first encounter, it would not be until January 1, 1981, that I would hear from Perley again. He called to wish me a Happy New Year. The conversation was not long, but I believed that was the beginning of our beautiful romance.

       Love,
       Valerie

Perley Takes a Risk

Tingleys was planning a sleigh ride and I really didn't want to go alone. So I finally got up the nerve and decided to call Valerie, but deep down I thought she would never want to go with me. She was really pretty and so nice; I convinced myself that she wouldn't want to go out with me, but I barrelled ahead and called her. We chatted on the phone for a while and finally I asked her to the sleigh ride by saying, "Tingleys is having a sleigh ride; you wouldn't want to go, would you?" To my surprise Valerie said, "Oh, I would love to." I thought for sure she was going to say, "No." We went on the sleigh ride. I discovered she liked Chinese food so we went out to dinner the next night. We went out on a date every night for ten evenings, and I finally said, "Would you like to go steady?" Valerie replied, "I thought we were."

My relationship with Valerie was magic from the beginning. We always encourage and love one another. I guess it was the magic of our lives, and how my life had taken such a positive turn when I met Valerie.

Our First Date—Valerie

On February 8, 1981, Perley and I went on a sleigh ride out on the Hanwell Road. It was a cold brisk night and everyone on the sleigh ride huddled together under the blankets we brought. Perley and I had a wonderful time that night. It was a night that I will always remember. I looked forward to seeing Perley again.

Birthday Cake February 10, 1981

Just two days after the sleigh ride, it was Perley's thirty-eighth birthday. I made a birthday cake and invited him over. When Perley saw the cake, he started crying. It was then I realized that there was more to Perley and all his laughter. He demonstrated being a very sensitive and caring man, and I fell in love with this very gentle man. We began dating and grew closer every day. It was magic for sure.

How Holly Helped Perley

When I first met Valerie, I was so up against it. I was dirt poor. I had lost my house and basically everything I had. All I had left was the shirt on my back, and a wreck of a car that I didn't know if it would last me throughout the day. Life took a really big turn when I met Valerie, and a man by the name of Holly Albright who lived across the street from Valerie. When I started going with Valerie, I met Holly and his wife, Olive. Holly seemed to take a liking to me and became a great friend and a wise mentor.

Holly was an older man. I had only known him a couple of weeks, but I knew he cared about me. Shortly after I met him, he said, "That old car isn't going to last you too long." He told me that he knew a fellow down the road that sold cars by the name of Bob Craig. He thought we should go down and talk to Bob and see what he had for a vehicle. I didn't like to tell Holly that I didn't have a cent to my name and that I couldn't afford a car. I was just

Olive and Holly

trying to get my life back on track financially. I guess Holly knew that anyway. We went down to see the cars, and there was this beautiful Comet; oh, it was so beautiful. So we jumped in the car and went for a long drive. When we got back, Holly said, "How do you like the car?" I told him I loved it and explained that I couldn't afford it at that time, and that Bob would have other cars in later on. Holly turned to Bob and said, "Will you take my cheque?" I couldn't believe this was happening to me. Holly turned to me and said, "Perley, you can pay me back when you get the money. If you don't get the money, don't worry about it." No one had ever done anything like that for me. I just could not believe Holly had just bought me a car.

I worked hard and got the money saved to pay him back. When I did take the money to Holly, I almost had to fight with him to take the money back. We lived on Perley Avenue when Valerie and I got married and we lived there for about five years, and were great neighbours with Holly and Olive. We sold that house and moved, but I always went back to visit Holly. I took him berry picking, apple picking, and down river to get vegetables at the stands. Everywhere we went, he wanted to pay the bill. Being the produce manager at the grocery store, we bought fruits and vegetables from all these people, and they would say, "Oh, Perley, we can't take your money." Holly would tease me and say that I was the only man he knew that my money was no good. We would have a great laugh and spent quality time together.

Holly Albright was a very special person. He was like the dad I never had and Holly helped me get back on my feet. I will always remember the kindness that was shown to me by Holly. Holly's kindness, Valerie's love, and all my friends brought me to a deeper knowledge of who I am, and my self-esteem blossomed along with my career.

Perley and the Blended Family

I was always close to my children even after my divorce. I kept in contact with them and paid child support the whole time until they graduated. When the last one graduated, my ex-wife told me I didn't have to pay any more support. I appreciated the fact that she was very fair when it came to the financial agreement we had. I always stay connected to my children and I feel extremely close to my children. I talk to my son, Michael, every day and my two daughters, Faye and Kelly, weekly. I just love my children so much and Valerie has been so kind to my children and they love her, too. Valerie has one son, Theodore who is a minister. He lives over north with his wife and family, and she has one daughter Patricia. Of course, they all have children so we have lots of grandchildren. Families have changed so much from when I was young. Way back families did a lot more together. Nowadays computers, iPads, and all the new technology have changed the concept of families so much. We still stay as close and connected to our family as possible. I love them all so much. After three years of "dating" and loving each other, Valerie and I got married.

Back Row: Bill and Roger Ross.
3rd Row (L-R): Gayle, Zena (Mom), Elaine Ross.
2nd Row: Val and Perley.
Front Row: Mike and Angela Ross.

June 2, 1984: Perley and Valerie's Wedding Day—Valerie Gives the Details

We were married in the Nazarene Church by Pastor Rick Doige. Our good friends, John and Shirley Schriver, stood up with us. We had a lovely breakfast buffet at the Lord Beaverbrook Hotel. A highlight of the buffet was Rick's wife, Linda, singing, "*Something Beautiful.*"

> Something beautiful, something good
> All my confusion He understood
> All I had to offer Him was brokenness and strife
> But he made something beautiful of my life
> If there ever were dreams
> That were lofty and noble
> They were my dreams at the start
> And hope for life's best were the hopes
> That I harbor down deep in my heart
> But my dreams turned to ashes
> And my castles all crumbled, my fortune turned to loss
> So I wrapped it all in the rags of life
> And laid it at the cross.
>
> *Author Unknown* (AllTheLyrics.com, n.d.)

The song said it all for us as we began our lives together.

The Honeymoon

Our first night of married life was spent in the honeymoon suite at the Pres du Lac Motel in Grand Falls, NB. We left Grand Falls and headed to Ontario. We stopped at Cornwall, Ontario, spent the night and the next morning we headed for Guelph where Perley's brother, Ivan, and his wife, Janet, lived. Then the four of us headed to Niagara Falls. After a long and lovely day, we headed back to Guelph and stayed overnight with Ivan and his family. We left our car at Ivan's and he drove us to the Toronto Airport and then we were off to Edmonton, Alberta. We picked up a rental car so that we could visit special spots and visit our good friends, Dan and Shirley McKinley who were living in Jasper.

While we were enjoying the province, Perley had a brush with death. It happened as we were driving along and all of a sudden there were two baby bear cubs. They were so adorable that Perley wanted to stop and get closer to them. Out of the car he goes and scrambles up the hill to get a close-up picture. All of a sudden, the massive mama bear rose up out of the grass. I never saw anyone run so fast. Perley turned grey and I saw him shaking as he darted to our car. That is my Perley though–always adventurous and daring. Perley is a man full of courage and love.

Love you,
Valerie

Perley's Desire to Become a Magician Grows

Many years ago, Valerie and I went on a trip to Las Vegas, and we were walking down the street when I spied a magic store. I told Valerie to go on ahead, and I was going to go over to that store. I ended up staying in that store for almost two hours. The room was full of magic tricks and I purchased about five or six of them. I was excited and the tricks didn't cost much. The next time I was asked if I had any more tricks after doing the quarter trick, I would always say, "Oh yes, I have another one right here." The kids just loved it and I loved putting a smile on their faces.

One day a friend asked me if I would go to his daughter's birthday party. I told him that I was a little old for that. He said, "No, I mean to do some magic tricks." I said, "No, no they wouldn't want to see that." He told me they would love it so I went to the party. When I arrived, they had a little table set up for me and I put my tricks on the table, and started performing, and wow, their eyes got so big. I think they thought I was Houdini. That is how I began performing for the children. My interest in magic and making children smile really grew that day. When I began to go into the community and some schools, our granddaughter recalls one trick that did a backflip.

Magic by Janelle Peters

My grandfather is an amazing man. I have great memories of time spent with him when I was younger. I remember my first experience on a motorcycle was with my grandfather. I felt so safe with him. It was so much fun and exhilarating. My grandfather came to my school to do magic and I always felt so proud to tell my friends he was my grampy. They wouldn't always believe me and it sometimes would turn into a silly argument trying to make them believe that I had a celebrity for a grandfather. He wasdoing a magic show for my school one time and his cup and water trick went wrong. He accidently dumped (at least I think it was) water on my teacher's head. It was hilarious. We all had a good laugh and the show carried on as if it was supposed to happen that way.

    Some of my favorite memories with my grandfather are the times we spent playing pool and ping pong. He played so good and seldom let me win; they were great times. My grandfather is fond of ice-cream and Blue Jays baseball games and so am I. I am 31 years old now and the great memories of my childhood with my grandfather will last a lifetime. I love him dearly and I am so proud to call him Grampy. My 9-year-old daughter, Addyson, has an amazing bond with him as he was really her first father figure. She lights up when she sees him and I know she feels the same excitement I did when I was a child. It is pretty special to have someone so "cool"–like a magician for a Grampy! We love you so much.

                                            Janelle

Janelle

Chris and Janelle

Perley's Magic Spreading

I remember another time I did a magic show at a wedding in Saint John. Normally, I felt comfortable and prepared, but when I walked into this reception, I felt uncomfortable. Everyone was high falutin'; I mean tuxedoes and dressed very formal. There were some of the Irvings, the Mayor, and it was a huge event. I wondered why they wanted little 'ol me to perform. They had reserved a beautiful room for me and all my meals were paid for. I felt so out of place and was feeling really weird. I got my show all set up in the corner. I heard the announcement that I was going to perform. The MC asked everyone to sit down, and all I could think of was, I am never going to get a smile on their faces. It was the first time I remember feeling that way. I just was myself and performed the best I could. When I was done, they were in tears; they were laughing so hard. So many came up and told me how much they enjoyed my show. That wedding event gave me a real confidence boost in my magic career.

Perley and Mr. Jack Irving.

Who would ever believe that John (Jack) Irving himself would request my magic show at all of their annual events for many years, right up until his death. Jack and I became great friends, and I was elated to receive a personal letter from his son after his dad's passing.

John E. Irving, CM ([Order of Canada], January 1, 1932–July 21, 2010), was a Canadian businessman, the youngest son of the industrialist, K. C. Irving. Born in NB, Jack Irving (as he was called), along with his brothers, J. K. and Arthur, and their three families shared the ownership and operating responsibility for what is known informally as the Irving Group of Companies.

Jack Irving gained a reputation as being the most reflective of the Irving family and was known for being far less aggressive than his older brothers when it came to business, choosing instead to listen intently and leave the talking to them. Many credit this to a kidnapping incident in 1982. Though he was found unharmed, the kidnapping left him aware of his own mortality and a shift in his personality was noted. Jack was a humble and kind man, especially to me.

Having the respect and honour of working my magic for the Irving family was a wonderful experience for me.

Now I am going to take you on a little journey with my magical friends that I have met over the years.

Perley at an Irving picnic.

The Magician's Tributes

Magician June Anstee Meets 'Perley the Magician' Palmer

John and Eileen Lamb.

We arrived in Canada some 10 years ago. My husband and I were taken to our very first yard sale by our daughter. We were fascinated by the items being offered, and then we noticed a group of people gathered around a gentleman performing magic tricks. Having recently retired as a professional lady magician, we were both fascinated by the fun and laughter that was being created. We introduced ourselves and learned that this gentleman was none other than Perley the Magician, an all-time favourite entertainer with the people of Fredericton.

After our initial meeting, Perley had to admit that he had never met a lady magician before and was anxious to meet up and talk magic as soon as possible. Just two hours later, Perley and his lovely wife, Valerie, arrived on our doorstep and, within a short period of time, we became very great friends. Perley and I shared our careers and discussed many forms of magic. The four of us had a great visit and knew it would be a lifelong friendship.

Entertaining people is an art: The Number 1 priority is to have a good personality in order to succeed in this magician career. There is no shortcut to becoming a professional entertainer. Once a decision is made on what form of entertainment you wish to pursue, be prepared for a challenging time ahead. On the surface, it would appear to be a glamorous occupation, but to be really successful, you have to spend countless hours perfecting your craft.

Over the years, the art has grown in popularity. Many large-scale illusions have been created by Americans; however, the art of magic is universal.

Magic is appreciated by all age groups; the popularity of this form of entertainment is clearly evident by the number of parents that book magicians for children's parties. Likewise, close-up magic is very popular when considering entertainment at corporate events and wedding parties.

Fredericton is well-served in this respect by Perley the Magician, a wonderful and professional man who has perfected his craft. He has a great personality and can be guaranteed to bring a smile to the faces of young and old alike. We are proud to have Perley and his wife, Valerie, as our friends.

Eileen (June) and John Lamb

Tribute From Magician Brent Cairns

In 1990, when I was attending the Perfect Magic annual convention in Montreal, I met my long-time friend and magician, Perley. I was waiting to attend the famous Dan Garrett lecture, when a soft-spoken, curly haired gentleman sat down beside me. He introduced himself as Perley Palmer and proceeded to perform small miracles with coins, handkerchiefs, and even more. From that moment on, I have been best friends with this great guy. He invited me and my girlfriend and now wife, Linda, to visit him and his wife in Fredericton. That summer, Linda and I drove to Fredericton for a little vacation. Perley and Val would not let us stay in a hotel–they graciously let us stay in their home. Perley and I would practice our magic tricks for each other and discuss the latest magic effect we were working on. We would practice until the wee hours of the night. I remember waking up and looking out the bedroom window, only to see Perley washing my car and scrubbing the bug guts off the front. We stayed a couple of days and became best friends even to this day. Over the years, we have attended many magic conventions and I always look forward to seeing my friend, Perley.

Brent Cairns

                Your friend and magician colleague,
                Brent Cairns

Tribute From Magician Chris Lovely

My name is Chris Lovely. I believe I had a role in Perley's life and he had a huge role in mine.

I met Perley in my mid-teens. Just prior to the meeting, I had discovered magic and had seen him perform. I went and spoke with him after the show and had a million questions to ask him. He answered them all and didn't seem annoyed for even a second. Shortly after that, I started helping him with his shows, setting them up and helping him tear down. He gave me my first paying gig by allowing me to perform at his magic booth at the annual Fredericton Exhibition. He always encouraged me and told me, with practise, I could do magic for a living. That is exactly what happened. I now perform magic professionally. Perley had the most wonderful way of giving me a new magic trick as a gift without just saying, "here is a new trick." He would give me a trick and say, "Hey, Chris, I'm having trouble mastering this trick. Would you take it home and work on it for me." A week or so later, I would perform it for him, and if he saw it was a trick that I really enjoyed, he would say, "Ah, I'll never get that. Why don't you just keep it, Chris."

I would say Perley is the main reason I became so interested in magic and stuck with it. He is very talented and can master so many

Perley and Chris Lovely.

tricks. I finally got a chance to see him again at a magic convention in Las Vegas. Although it had been about 20 years since we had worked together, it was like no time has passed at all. My memories of him are filled with joy and excitement as I learned more and more magic. Perley is a great man that has had a major impact on my life.

                Your magician friend for life
                Chris

A Tribute From Mike D'Urzo-Mega Magic

I had the pleasure of working with Perley at the Fredericton Exhibition in 2016. We had an absolute blast performing together in the "Magic Tent." Being a professional magician for over fifteen years, I had such a great time watching Perley's show throughout the week. Each performance made me laugh harder each time. He has such a great personality both on and off stage. His magic is mind blowing and his comedy is amazing.

I don't often work with other magicians, but it was a real treat being able to perform on the same stage as Perley. He even taught my fiancé, Mariam, a cool card trick, which even fooled me! As I walked through the exhibition midway, I could not believe that EVERYONE knew Perley–a true celebrity! He was always so happy to share a trick with anyone who came by.

I hope that our paths will cross again in the future. It's not every day that I meet someone with so much love and passion for what they do–true magic!

Mike D'Urzo.

Wishing you all the best my friend—until we meet again.

Mike

A Tribute From David Johnson, the Magician

If it were not for Perley, I would not be the person or professional that I am today. As a mentor and friend, he always offers the very best of who he is and that speaks incredible volumes. I often reflect on our times together and Perley's love of entertaining and his appreciation of life. I am elated for his health, success, and this publication.

      Love you, Perley.
      David

David Johnson

Perley Concludes

I have had the opportunity to do shows at Sunday schools, day cares, birthdays, weddings, family reunions, company parties, and malls. This has been wonderful for me and has made me a household name in my province, especially my community. I really enjoy magic and watching the faces of the people light up. Some of the expressions on people's faces are just unreal.

Doing a show at a wedding is always fun and I get to wear my tuxedo and dress right up. I look really spiffy. People are always so happy at weddings and it is a great feeling to see people's smiles wider than normal. It is really elating. I also love doing children's shows. I have been blessed to have so many friends over the years, which helped launch my magician career.

A Tribute to Perley Palmer-Dow Johnston

It is a pleasure and an honour to say a few words about one of my best friends, Perley Palmer, or as he is affectionately called, "The Magic Man." We first met years ago when he was an employee of Tingley's Save Easy store in Nashwaaksis. He was usually the first employee you would see when you entered the store. I remember him introducing himself and entertaining me and others who were gathering nearby. He always did two or three of his many magic tricks. We all realized that this man was a professional magician. I remember thinking that this was a great way to welcome customers into the store. I have always been impressed with Perley's magic skills and his friendly mannerisms. I purchased groceries at the store for many years, primarily to have a chat with Perley and to be dazzled by his tricks. We have been best friends all these years.

My son, Jim, and I attended one of Perley's magic shows. There was a large crowd there, both young and old. Perley noticed me and invited Jim and I up to the stage to be an assistant with a magic trick. Jim was so excited about being part of Perley's show: It made him feel important and helpful at the same time. Perley's gesture gave Jim's self-esteem a huge boost. Jim was mentally and physically challenged and had few good friends. Perley filled the void that Jim had with his unconditional love and attention. Jim told me more than once that Perley was his best friend and was like a brother he never had.

I remember one Christmas: Perley and his dear wife, Valerie, came to the house and put on an entire magic show for Jim, his sisters, mother, and me. He wouldn't accept any money and just said, "We wish you, Jim, and your family a Merry Christmas and a great New Year." What a gift!

Jim was absolutely thrilled when Perley would take him for a ride on his beautiful Honda Motorcycle. When Perley came into our home, Jim would rush to the door and say, "Hi Perley, are you going to take me for a ride on your motorcycle?" Perley would smile and say, "Yes buddy, let's go." They would go on long rides, and Perley always made sure they stopped somewhere along the way for a treat. Perley took Jim for many bike rides over the years and he was always so kind and thoughtful. For our Jim, I am sure these were his happiest memories. Jim passed away when he was only 45 years old. His short life was made a lot brighter due to the time Perley spent with him. We are forever grateful for these memories.

At this present time, my friend, Perley, is fighting for his life. He faces this terrible disease and diagnosis of cancer head on, with no regrets and a positive attitude. He says he will continue making people a little happier as long as he can. Perley is at our local market every Saturday morning doing his magic and meeting with all the people–just to put a smile on their face. This is the way Perley is. I am amazed at the reception he gets when he meets people. He can go almost anywhere in the city, and someone will always come forward; give him a big hug and say, "I love you, Perley." This speaks volumes for the way he is admired, loved, and respected by the general public. Thank you, Perley, for the numerous times you have and continue to bring joy, fun, and excitement to my family and many others. You and Valerie are in my thoughts and prayers.

        Honoured to be your friend, Perley
        Dow

Tributes: The Many Friends, Businesses, and Colleagues of Perley, the Magician

Fredericton Police Force

-Leanne J. Fitch, Chief of Police/Chef de Police M.O.M.

On behalf of the Fredericton Police Force, I extend a sincere thank-you to Perley for his many loyal years of support. Perley is a beloved character that has entertained our police family for years and has brought smiles and delight to young and old alike. Perley's enthusiasm, optimism, great heart, and humor are treasures and, while he often tells people that the police family is dear to him, I can tell you that he is dear to us in return.

Leanne J. Fitch

-Staff Sergeant Paul Babtiste

Fredericton Police Force Officers with Perley - Paul Babtiste (left), Steve Cliff (right)

I met Perley in 1998 when he was doing magic tricks at the kids' Christmas party for the Fredericton Police Force, which he has been doing for 27 years. I instantly noticed how he captured his intended audience of children, but quickly realized he also captivated the adults. I could see the adults laughing and joking as they watched and see the smiles on their faces. Perley has a way of holding our attention and bringing us to a place that is very rewarding.

I see Perley once or twice a year performing at our police parties, and also at the local schools, markets, and even on the streets, wherever and whenever he had an opportunity to bring joy and happiness to anyone who sees him: It does not have to be a big audience where the show was preplanned and Perley had been hired to perform his magic. He works his magic on anyone at any time oftentimes and not for money. Perley's desire is to simply bring happiness to all those who have the pleasure to see him. What a true gift for one to have!

Through the years, I would continue to see Perley on occasion performing for all the kids as he always did. Eventually, I had my own children, Hannah and Olivi. I saw my children experience the joy and happiness Perley delivers.

I simply thought of Perley as an acquaintance, as someone with whom I would speak when we saw each other, but nothing more–at least, that is what I thought! Then, in early 2015, I was working at the police station when I heard that our Perley "the Magician" was quite sick with cancer and his diagnosis was not favorable. I remember hearing the news and instantly felt myself tearing up. I felt as if I just learned that a close family member had died. I was a wreck. I remember getting in my police car and leaving the police station trying to find a place to park to compose myself. I didn't realize until that moment how much Perley meant to me. He was a mentor and someone I looked up to without ever acknowledging it. I immediately found a phone number for Perley and called him up. I later met Perley at the Northside Market where he was again performing. I walked towards Perley in uniform and admired his strength and courage as he continued to bring happiness to everyone around him. He was much stronger than the man wearing the uniform that day and I admired Perley for his outlook on life. He shared some personal moments with me that day and gave me a new look on life, for which I will forever be in his debt. Perley also shared one of his card tricks with me and asked that I carry it on for him. He wanted me to have a piece of him to remember.

Perley, you are a true man, a true inspiration, a mentor, someone who throughout your life has impacted so many in a positive way. If the rest of us could only learn to practice a portion of what you represent and your true desire to be there for others, this world would be a better place to live.

Take care of yourself, my friend. I look forward to many more tricks from you!

Paul Babtiste

-Karla Forsythe

Perley's magic tricks impacted our son Jordan when he was about 12 years old. As a result of seeing one of his shows, Jordan went on to learn several magic tricks. He became so efficient at them that he was asked to perform at Steve Cliff's daughter's birthday party. Jordan is now 24 years old and can still perform the same tricks. ☺ Thank you, Perley.

-The Character of Our Friend, Perley Palmer: Tribute by Steve, Karen, Amber, and Chelsea Cliff

Since my children were little, we have seen Perley, the Magician on numerous occasions, such as at Christmas parties, birthday parties, and shows at the Northside Market and the Fredericton Exhibition. All those were great shows and my daughters loved every minute, but the times they and I remember most are the casual encounters where we have met Perley at the grocery store, out for breakfast at the Sunshine Diner, or in the Fredericton Mall as he was shopping with his lovely wife. Each time, Perley took a minute to speak to my girls and I, perform a couple quick magic tricks for our entertainment, and share a laugh. These are the times when we most remember the bright light shining from Perley's great personality and character. Perley is truly loved by our family.

-Andrew Frizzell, Age 7

My favorite part of Perley performing is when he turns his head with that box . . . it's so cool!!!

-Jerett Blackmore

I have many great memories from my childhood and Perley, the Magician is certainly included in them. Perley always performed at the police children's Christmas party every year and my friends and I would gather around and try our best to figure out his tricks. I now bring my son to the same Christmas party and nothing has changed, Perley continues to bring joy and amazement to children of all ages!

                        Your friend,
                        Jerett Blackmore

-Bruce, Age 9

He's a nice magician and stuff.

-Ben, Age 8

He's really good at being funny when burning his wallet.

-Lily, Age 4

When he was doing magic, his magic wand broke . . . and it had a string inside so it didn't fall.

-Tribute From Denis Vanember

I don't have a real elegance for emotional stories, but here is my best memory of Perley: My wife and I were taking our son to Open Farm Day several years ago in South Hampton. We got on a wagon ride and my son, Bruce (Age 6 at the time), immediately recognized one of the other passengers who was sharing the ride with us. It was Perley who was enjoying the day with his own family. Despite the fact it was clearly Perley's day off and he had no obligation to the children present on the wagon, Perley made no hesitation to pull out many props from his sleeves and pockets and put on an impromptu magic show. When he spoke to my son in this intimate atmosphere, he spoke as if he knew Bruce and had known him all of Bruce's life (though I'm sure of the thousands of kids Perley deals with, he had no memory of my son). We've done this wagon ride yearly many times, but no year sticks out more in my family's memory then the day we got to share a ride with Perley, the Magician.

-Tribute From Scott Patterson

Years ago when Perley moved in down the street, my daughters Robyn (7 years) and Erin (5 years) came running up the street with their friends screaming, "Daddy, Daddy!!! The best thing in the world has happened." As I watched the four or five girls all high fiving and hugging almost to the point of tears with excitement, I asked what was so great? The response was,

"Perley Dad, Perley!!! He lives on our street now." They spent the rest of the summer casually walking past his house hoping to see something disappear, catch fire, or explode. A few days later, my girls saw me outside speaking with Perley's wife and, when I later explained who she was, all they could say was, "Lucky, I wish I was married to Perley, I bet it's awesome."

I came to the conclusion that if Santa Claus had moved in next door and rented rooms to the Easter bunny and Tooth Fairy. It would have been a pale comparison to the "super, awesome, wonderful Perley" (actual quote) down the street.

-Andrew Miller, 50

If Perley got a nickel for every smile he put on someone's face, he would be the richest man on earth.

-Judy McCarty

What comes to my mind about Perley is the first time I saw him wasn't so much about how he impacted me, but it was the look on the children's faces, the delight in their eyes, and smiles bigger than the moon. He truly turns us into children when he performs, and brings us adults back to a safe and wonderful place. What a talent to have!

-Olivia Babtiste, Age 10

He's funny, he's nice, and he does good magic tricks. I could never figure out how he gets his wallet to catch fire. ☺

-Hannah Babtiste, Age 13

He makes everyone laugh! And I like his twirly, whirly, Perley hair!

Emily Beck, daughter of FPF Officer Dave Beck

FPF-.Lft. Steve Cliff, Hannah Battiste, Perley, FPF-Paul Battiste

A Tribute From Brookside Mall Property Manager, Tim Woods

Further to my talks with Perley about writing something for his book, I have jotted down a few comments on my friend Perley. I arrived at the Brookside Mall as the property manager in 1989. Perley was there at the time selling prints and clocks in the mall corridor. He was one of the first persons I met. How could anyone who meets Perley not remember his genuine caring for people? First impressions are so important and this introduction created what has become a great 27-year friendship.

One of Perley's biggest assets is that he always has time for everybody, young and old. He loves children, but has a soft spot for people in general and it shows. It never mattered if he had sales or sold a hundred pieces of his handmade products, such as clocks; he would smile and laugh and do tricks for everybody. As he became more and more popular with his magic shows, he stopped selling products in the mall, but continued to be a regular working his magic. When he is here, you know it, because the customers are all smiling.

Over the years, Perley has become part of the mall. He has put on a March break show every year for as long as I can remember and has been assisting our friends Santa and the Easter Bunny on a regular basis. He is at times more popular than they are!!

The only place I believe that Perley's magic did not work was on the golf course. He told me it did though . . . and that is why my ball would go in the hole. Perley, the Magician–he is always the gentleman.

Perley and Tim Woods.

Your friend
Tim Woods

A Tribute From Jellystone Park NB: Janet and Peter Clark

We are honored to be asked to provide our appreciation for Perley, the Magician and what he means to all of us at Jellystone Park NB. Perley has brought joy and laughter to our campers at Jellystone Park in Woodstock, NB, for over 20 years now. Perley, the Magician has brought a sparkle to a child's eye so many times. Children and adults alike are amazed when they have a coin come out of their ear. There are the happy cheers from a large group of our Jellystone Park NB campers when something disappears before their eyes–it is really magic.

We have been so blessed with all of Perley's performances over the years. Perley always goes out of his way to accommodate our schedules and always gives a little pre-show in our camp store–to the delight of all the shoppers who happen to be there at the time. Perley is truly a "one of a kind" and he always puts 110% into everything he does! This is why we made him an honorary Park Ranger and now we affectionately call him Ranger Perley! Thank you, Perley, for all you do for everyone and the special magic you share with all ages! Jellystone Park NB loves Perley, the Magician and welcomes him with open arms every time he comes to visit!!

The FREX

This year, the biggest event I have done is the Fredericton Exhibition. Mike Vokey has been very kind to me. This is a big event with thousands of children and adults watching the magic over the week. I have been doing the magic show for 21 years at the exhibition, and I hope to do the show again this next year. Everett Porter, a retired policeman, has been a very good friend of mine at the exhibition and has helped me a lot. Everett and I go way back playing hockey and ball together. He always makes sure I get to the exhibition and get set up. Mike Vokey has been very generous and so kind to me throughout my years at the FREX as we call it.

A Tribute to my Friend, Perley, the Magician: Mike Vokey

To be recognized and appreciated in the community is a wonderful achievement. To be known for your talent as an entertainer and for the joy and laughter you bring to others is a blessing. To be acknowledged for the lifetime of contributions in the community and by the community is humbling. This is not a story about a great magician. This is a story about a great man.

I met Perley Palmer when I first moved to Fredericton to take the leadership of the Provincial Exhibition. What I remember most about the meeting was his sense of humor and his curly hair. Perley was quick to pull a card trick out from seemingly nowhere, and follow it up with a corny joke or two. My first impression of the man is as true today as it was then. He is a truly sincere person who has such a positive outlook on life that I am envious of.

I remember that first meeting. Perley took out a deck of cards and performed a trick as smooth as any magician could. Afterwards he broke the magician's golden rule and did it again showing me how to do the trick myself. I clumsily performed the trick and he assured me that I would get better at it. He gave me the deck of cards to keep and told me to practice. Of course, I never have been able to do the trick with the sleight of hand like Perley, but it was the first of many tricks and magic props he would give me to try to teach me to perform. Perley is as generous as he is charismatic.

Perley creates magic and mesmerizes the audience. But it is a pantomime, and the audience knows that it's a ruse. It's in the name: a "magic trick." They play along when Perley tugs his sleeves to show there is nothing hidden within them, or when the top hat is empty of a rabbit, or eggs, or flowers. Beneath the façade, there is only sleight of hand, and misdirection at a key moment. Perley's strength is definitely misdirection. We think of Perley as a children's entertainer, but I have watched him perform for audiences a hundred times and, often, the adults and parents are as mesmerized as the kids are.

Perley's positive outlook and sense of humor would be put to the test following a visit to the doctor's office when he was diagnosed with Stage 4 cancer.

I am reminded of a story I heard about the amazing David Copperfield. Apparently a few years back, he was mugged in West Palm Beach. Yes, it's funny, when told to, "empty your pockets" and he pulled out a bunny rabbit. But it's also depressing. If someone who can make himself disappear isn't safe, who is? Likewise, I wonder if a magician like Perley can make this cancer disappear, and I am hoping that he can.

Perley hasn't been able to make the cancer disappear–yet, he is fighting it with his tenacity, courage, and great sense of humour. I hope that with the medical treatment, his positive spirit, and maybe a little magic, Perley's cancer will go into remission. I am just happy that Perley continues to make me laugh with jokes, wonder with his magic tricks, and also makes me happy to have him as my friend.

> Mike Vokey
> Executive Director
> NB Provincial Exhibition, EST 1827

A Tribute from Tim Gillies

Perley, Tim Gillies and Ralph Silliphant

My friendship with Perl, which is the name some of us have given him, goes back almost fifty years. I got to know him at Tingley's Save Easy. Perl always had a joke to tell or a trick to show my kids when they came along in the 1980s. Perl has a real genuine way about him and with people: He is truly one of a kind. He loves playing pool and he always beats me, but ping pong is a different story

Like everyone else in Fredericton, I was devastated by the news when Perl got sick. A few months after that, we would chat over a coffee. He still loved doing a trick or two for anyone at our table. At one of our coffee sessions, he gave me an autographed picture of himself and world famous magician David Copperfield–something I will always cherish. Thanks, Perl.

Tim Gillies-An old Friend

A Tribute from Gary Gordon

I remember the first time I met Perley. It was at Tingley's Save Easy, and I was making my first delivery to the produce department. Perley came out and gave me a really warm welcome.

Over the years we have become close. We have travelled to several cities together and shared so many laughs. When we returned from our excursions, we would share some of our stories with our wives and laugh all over again.

One of Perley's tricks is to hide on me while we are walking around a new city. I would look up and all around and I would backtrack and find him, behind a tree or lamp post, behind a wall, in an alley–you name it and we would have the biggest hoot about it. It never gets old.

I've helped Perley set up his swimming pool many times. One season, we really thought that we knew what we were doing and that was our first mistake. Everything was going smoothly. We had the water flowing into the pool and decided to go for a coffee. When we came back

Gary and Perley

we started to hook up the pump and filter. (There's about a foot of water in this 15-foot round pool by now). Anyway, Owen had joined us so the three of us couldn't figure out how to hook it onto the pool. It just wouldn't fit where it was supposed to. I was standing on the other side of the pool looking at them and suddenly, I said to them, "Boys, . . . I think the pool is inside out." Of course they didn't believe me until they looked for themselves. We laughed at our stupidity and then began to bail out the pool with buckets. We lifted the side of the pool to try to get the last 50 gallons out. We turned the pool right side out and began the filling process again. Laughing and shaking our heads.

The first year that we set up the pool, the ground was not level, so when the pool was filled, the water spilled over the lower side. One hot day, Perl was lounging on the lower part of the pool and with his added weight the pool let go, sending 500 gallons of water and Perley went ass over tea kettle, up against his new fence, and washing out the tomato garden. If the fence had not been there, Perley would have surely ended up in the woods. What a shocked look Perley would have had, and I would have loved to have been there to see it. It was a great story and I still think about how funny it would have been to see

I remember one time we were planning a trip to Montreal so Perley could buy some magic tricks. He left me in charge of booking the hotel. We were driving up in Perley's (new to him) van, because his old Buick had finally died. I got on the Internet and was looking at hotel prices, some were $565.00 per night! I found what I thought to be in the middle of St. Catherine's Street for $120.00 per night or $60.00 each. When we arrived we saw all these pink and white balloons strung across the street for about 12 blocks. We checked in and the room was clean and beds comfy. Looking out our window overlooking St. Catherine's Street, we saw a lot of men holding hands and a few others were necking. Going out into the street, Perley and I struck up a conversation with a chap and asked him what was going on here with all the balloons? He told us, this was the "Village-The Gay Village!" How was I supposed to know I had never been to Montreal before? Well, that was the biggest laugh we had, and it lasted our whole stay. It truly was a nice village.

The hotel owner had a keen eye on Perley's tricks. The owner was from India and was always curious about Magic and had a relentless desire to know how the tricks were accomplished. So Perley had to bring out the big guns to really baffle him.

Perley was looking for a special shirt that would baffle people with a lot of glitter. He checked out some stores, but there was nothing to be found so he asked around and was told there was a store about 12 blocks down where he could probably find what he was looking for. Perley was all excited. Low and behold when we got there it was "Value Village." We got a good laugh over this, but to no avail–he could not find a shirt that tickled his fancy.

All in all, we had a great trip. Lots of jokes, tricks, and pranks. Laughing all the way to and from, and that is how I always remember Perley–happy times.

                         Your friend,
                         Gordon

Perley Reflects

Reading these many wonderful memories and tributes makes me feel so blessed that I have touched so many lives in ways that I never realized. I am so grateful to have so many friends.

Perley and David Copperfield

Meeting the Mayor

I met the Mayor personally when I was performing at a New Year's Eve function at the Delta. Right as you go into the Delta, there is a huge area where people can congregate. Brad came up to me and said, "Perl, would you do me a really nice trick?" So I said, "Sure. "Everyone began to circle around me and I took a $20 bill out of my pocket and folded it up really small. I floated it into the air and walked about 5 feet away, while the bill was still floating. I walked back and said, "How did you like that?" Brad said, "I got you on this one. That was a trick bill." Brad took a $20 bill out of his pocket, folded it all up, and said, "Try floating this one." I did the same trick, and the bill floated. I met Brad a few days later and he told me, "I couldn't sleep that night trying to figure out how you did that trick." We had a good laugh over that trick, and it still makes me smile. Brad has always been a strong supporter of me and I appreciate him a lot. He is a good man and he was a wonderful Mayor of our city for many decades.

Tribute From Brad Woodside

My friendship with Perley goes back many years. I remember him greeting customers at Tingleys—he always had a trick or a story. It seemed to me he was having more fun than his customers; you could tell by his laugh. Perley loved to entertain and his magic got better and he always has a trick up his sleeve. Perley did magic shows for my kids. I watched as their little faces were fascinated and amazed and to see how much fun Perley was having was every bit as amazing. He has a real connection with people and I can't even imagine the number of birthday parties and magic shows Perley has done, but I'm sure it is a lot. When Perley was having health challenges, I thought it would be appropriate to have a special day set aside to honour Perley for the wonderful support he has given our communities for so long and an opportunity for a lot of us to say, "thanks, you're magical and loved by a lot of people."

       Your friend
       Brad

Proclamation Day

Well, Brad Woodside, our mayor, mentioned to me that there was going to be a little something coming up. I thought maybe a plaque or something like that. On the night I was asked to go to City Hall, I saw Gordon Burtt, Larry Atkinson, Joe Fisher, and a lot of people I knew. When Brad called me up and did the announcement that July 13 would be Perley Palmer day in the City of Fredericton—what a surprise! It was a huge honour and something I appreciate and am thankful for.

Mayor Brad Woodside announces Perley Palmer Day.
Picture submitted by *The Daily Gleaner*.

The evening was filled with an assortment of magic tricks, teary eyes, and a heartfelt speech given by Palmer.

"I would just like to take a moment to thank you wonderful people of Fredericton," said the local magician who has been performing magic shows across the province for more than 30 years.

After Monday night's ceremony, the 72-year-old said he was surprised when council announced the city would celebrate a day in his honour.

"I still can't believe it," said Perley who's going to celebrate his day by performing more magic tricks. "It'll be a special day."

Family and friends also came out to show their support Monday night, including his great-granddaughter Addyson who sat up front and watched as Perley performed a few magic tricks for Fredericton city council.

"He loves people, and it's nice to see it reflected back," said Valerie Palmer whose husband will often wake her up in the early hours of the morning to demonstrate a new magic trick he learned. "It's nice to see that people love him, too."

Three months ago, the local magician was diagnosed with Stage 4 prostate cancer, which has since travelled to his bladder, ribs, and tail bone–a shock to the couple who have been married for 31 years.

"He came back on April Fools' Day and we always play tricks on each other, and so he told me and I said, "This is not an good April Fools' joke, Perley," she said. "He said, 'Honey, I'm not joking," and I just went numb.

But, after receiving support from fans across New Brunswick and the entire country, Palmer said he plans to outlive the disease and is motivated by the survival stories he's heard from people who have shared their personal experiences with cancer.

"He's living his life and doing his magic and he has a positive attitude," she said, as her husband took pictures and hugged people during the meeting.

Mayor Brad Woodside said it's important to acknowledge Palmer's contribution to the community and said there has been a huge outpouring of support for him.

"One thing that you need when you're going through that is the feeling that the community supports you and, in this case, it's overwhelming," said Woodside who asked to be Palmer's assistant in upcoming magic shows.

After receiving his award, Perley was also greeted by members of the community, including Carol Deschenes. Palmer has been to three of her son's birthday parties, which are always a huge hit.

"We're going to celebrate every year, for sure," said the Fredericton resident. "I just came to say 'hello' to him. He has an amazing way with kids."

Palmer's love for magic started when he was visiting a magic store in Las Vegas.

Article from *The Daily Gleaner.*

Perley Palmer Day

Perley and Val surrounded by family—
Proclamation of Perley Palmer Day

We just celebrated the 3rd Annual Perley Palmer Day and boy was it ever fun. Juanita and Gary Gordon, along with many volunteers worked their heart out to make the day special for so many people—especially me. Thanks to all the volunteers!

Juanita and Gary

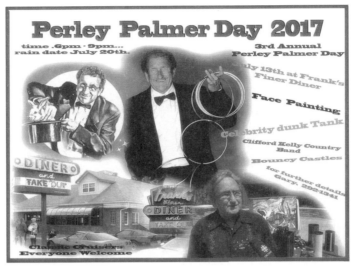

Poster by Tom Hiltz

Perley Palmer Day Celebrity Dunkers: (L-R) Jessie Yerxa and Karen Syroid

(L-R) Dr. Bonnie, Monica Antworth of the Canadian Cancer Society NB, Perley, Valerie and Roger

Our Community

When I am out and about and someone wants to see a magic trick, I always do one. I remember one time, Valerie and I were out at the buffet at the Silverwood Motel and this lady beckoned me over to their table and asked if I would do a trick for their son, which I did. Then there was another table with about five children. I did four or five tricks and everyone really enjoyed it. When we went to pay, the waitress told us that our meal was paid for by the people I had performed for. That used to happen a lot, and not that I do it for that, but it just happens. I remember one time we were at the Douglas Diner. We were done and paying the bill when the waitress said, "The bill has been paid for." I looked around and said, "There is no one here who paid for the meal?" She said, "I did. I've loved you since I was a little girl. You have always done tricks for me and I wanted to give something back." There have been so many special things and people like this throughout the years.

Life Changes—Owen Brewer–Memories

I remember when the Super Store realignment began, which involved moving Perley to a part-time position in the grocery department, which Perley decided was not for him. An offer from Saint Mary's Super Store was something Perley jumped on and off he went. Perley was a big draw for any store, and many customers just came to see or say, "Hello" to Perley. His departure left a huge hole in the store and our hearts. We missed him—everyday.

About a year after Perley left, I began to have problems with my heart. I had a major heart emergency and ended up spending about six months in the hospital, and I am sure Perley came to visit me almost every day. Some visits were long and some were short, but each one cheered me up. About a year and a half after my health issues, I started going everywhere with Perley when he did his magic shows. After all, I was the one who helped figure them out.☺ I really enjoyed seeing the expressions on people's faces—both children and adults—when Perley did his magic.

Travelling along with Perley took us to every corner of the province. Some of the places Perley was invited to be a guest, neither of us had been to, nor even heard tell of before. Imagine—in our own province. Perley was also invited to Prince Edward Island and Nova Scotia, and it was always an adventure. The one thing I was always sure of was that if there was no lunch at the show, Perley would always make sure we stopped at a nice restaurant, and we had an excellent meal. Perley always cared and helped people.

Perley—I love this guy! He would give you the shirt off his back—do anything for you. He was always there for me, and I want to do anything I could and can to repay him for his years of loyalty to me.

This last year has been very hard on both of us. Perley with his cancer diagnosis and I received a heart transplant. The one thing I missed was being the chauffer for Perley, but I am ready to accompany him on many more trips and seeing more country as Perley performs his magic.

Perley kept a positive attitude and stayed strong through his chemotherapy and treatment. He was so funny and showed great courage, when he received his chemotherapy in the morning and performed a magic show in the afternoon. Even though the doctor would tell Perley to take it easy for a couple of days, he kept his promise to put on a magic show for a child's birthday the same afternoon as the chemotherapy. Perley didn't want to let anyone down, that is how Perley has always been. This is probably why he is fighting this cancer and doesn't ever give up.

Keep up the great work; I am looking forward to going to many more magic shows and trips with you, my friend. Keep fighting and stay strong, which I am sure you will.

What a great friend you have been to me, and I will always be here for you.

>Love you, Perley—stay well.
>Owen Brewer

Retiring

I retired from the grocery business when I was seventy, just three years ago. At that time, I was working for St. Mary's Grocery store. St. Mary's Retail is located at St. Mary's First Nation on Fredericton's north side. I loved working for the manager; what I loved most is what he promised me is what I got, and he never went back on his word. When I started working at St. Mary's, I heard they were looking for a produce manager, and I told them I knew the perfect guy–my brother, Roger. He got the job and we were back working together again. We both finished up work after about ten years at St. Mary's. They were very nice to work for and I still have lots of friends there. Actually, one of the guys I worked with brought me a bunch of moose meat this past week. I still drop in the store and visit when I can.

Nathan Paul and Perley

Cancer Diagnosis

Well, it all started with pain in my tailbone. A week or so went by and it still hurt to sit down. Valerie said, "You better go to the doctor and get that checked." I waited another week or so and then made an appointment. Valerie and Pat came with me. I went to my family doctor first and was told there was a problem. I was referred immediately to a cancer doctor in town who ordered a bone scan and did a biopsy. I was told I would have to come back for the results in a day or two. When I went back, the doctor said things were not good and that it was cancer. He explained that the cancer had started out in my prostate, spread to some organs, my bowel, and was in my rib bones. Things did not look good. It hit me pretty hard. I went home and I started thinking about my funeral and who I would get to be pallbearers and things like that. The diagnosis came on April 1, but it was no April fool's joke.

Valerie Recalls the Cancer Diagnosis on April 1, 2015

On April 1, 2015, we were presented with the biggest challenge in our married life; Perley was diagnosed with Stage 4 Advanced Cancer, which had spread to some organs and his bones. Since the diagnosis, Perley has been taking Lupron injection–Leuprorelin, marketed under the brand name Lupron among others.

Perley is also receiving a variety of infusions that include receiving fluids and medication through the vein intravenously. Certain types of drugs and treatments to help with bone strengthening and, to date, a variety of medicines have been used in Perley's cancer treatment. In November 2016, Perley started chemo pills. This is a new part of our medical and life journey and one which we will walk through hand in hand—as always.

Perley Moves Forward

I am trying to deal with the diagnosis and not dwell on the fact that I have cancer. I have to stay cheerful and not to let it get me down. I go to the hospital about once a month. I go to the fourth floor and try and do a show for the people there, and try and remember all the beautiful people God has put in my path—people like Amy.

There is one special girl from Minto who has been a big part of my magic. Her name is Amy Doucette. Amy had cancer when she was a little girl and she took an awful shine to me. Of course, I thought a lot of her and did some special shows for her when she was fighting cancer. I noticed many times when I was doing a show that Amy's mother would bring her to see me perform. She was a dear little friend. Amy beat the cancer and she actually invited me to her graduation. I was away that day and could not go, but we talk periodically and she called when she heard I had cancer. Amy went into nursing, and I hope to see her soon to see where she is working and just catch up. Some people you never forget and Amy is one of them.

A Loving Tribute From Amy Lee Doucette

Hello, my name is Amy Lee Doucette. I am the 23-year-old daughter of Michael and Stacey (Logue) Doucette. I was diagnosed with a malignant Stage 4 cancer tumour at Age 4 on October 13, 1997. I did four sets of chemotherapy, two at the IWK Health Center and two at the Dr. Everett Chalmers Hospital.

Perley and I go back a long time. My parents took me to his magic show in Minto, NB, in 1998. I really enjoyed his show and, after the show, I had my picture taken with him. He was talking with my parents who told Perley how lucky I was to be even be able to enjoy the show today and he said, "Oh, how come?" My mom explained that I was just finishing up my last chemotherapy in January 1998. He then hugged me and

Amy and Perley

and squeezed me tight and said, "You're my girl." From that day forward, Perley and I have been pretty good friends and I am to this day—his girl.

When I turned six, my mom wanted to have a big birthday party for me. My mom contacted Perley to make sure he was able to do my party that we were having at a community hall in Minto, NB. He said nothing was going to stop him from being there. He said, "I will be there for my girl." Then we told Perley we invited all the students of the kindergarten classes and their siblings, roughly around 100 kids. I had to invite that many kids as I knew what it felt like being left out of things as I was different than other kids growing up.

I never wanted to leave kids out of parties or anything. Of course, my birthday is in January so the day of the party we had every kind of weather that you can: rain, snow, freezing rain, and sun. We were concerned that Perley was not going to make it.

A van pulls up and who walks through the door of the hall and says, "I made it here for my special girl." This was the best birthday party ever. He had a blast and so did all the kids. Throughout the years, Perley entertained at different events and we always try to attend them.

One time, after his event, I remember Perley telling me he had a motorbike and I said to him, "Someday I sure would love to go for a drive on your motorbike." Well, guess who went home and came back with an extra helmet and the motorbike? Yup, you're right: It was Perley and so off we went for a drive. When we got back, I looked at my mom; she looked so scared. Perley said, "What you thought—I was not going to bring my girl back to you?" My mom said, "Well, you just never know, but you would not keep her very long—she would drive you crazy. LOL."

Throughout the years, Perley and I stayed in contact the best we could even if it was seeing him at one of his magic shows in the mall or even if it was getting invited to a party. Even a couple of times, we had lunch together. I think the world of Perley and, when I heard the news about Perley being diagnosed with cancer, I was very sad. I do remember saying to Perley, "Look at me; I was strong and stubborn and, Perley, you are strong and can be stubborn, too. You can beat this." I also said, "When you're having a rough day, go in your wallet and pull out my picture and look at it and that will give you strength as you always said, "I can't believe what my girl went through." I will always be Perley's special girl and I think the world of Perley.

When Perley found out I was going to take nursing, he was so proud of me. Well, it is hard to believe that I just finished in June 2016. Two years at NBCC in St. Andrews where I studied the Practical Nurse course. I found out on November 1, 2016, that I am now a licensed practical nurse and Perley is so proud of me. When he heard the news that I passed, Perley said, "That's my girl. I am so proud of you."

Love you, Perley
Amy

Perley Reflects

Well, when I look back over my life, I thank God for the beautiful people He has brought into it, especially my wife, Valerie. She has helped unite and love all my friends and especially our families. Reading the tributes from my children and friends makes me cry every time because they are all so beautiful: I love them all and am so grateful for my family. I wanted to share my families' tributes to close off my story–for now. It is the love of my family and friends, and the prayers of so many people, along with great doctors, that have brought me to the particular point in my life. God willing, I will live to see their lives richly blessed as well.

Val and Perley

I went to visit my mom in Victoria a few weeks back with my good friend, Gary Gordon. I hadn't seen my mom in six or seven years. I knew if I didn't go that she might not be here for me to visit and I would always regret that. It was a long plane ride and my butt hurt for days from sitting so long, but it is worth it. I went and I am glad I did. She was so happy to see me. She couldn't get out of bed on her own. They had this contraption that lifted her out of bed and into her wheelchair. She could scoot around in that. Her memory is fine and we talked about things that happened 50 years ago. She was so happy to see me; she must have said, "I can't believe you're here" 50 times. Mom was so proud of me and introduced me to all the staff. Of course, I had several tricks up my sleeve and was always being asked by a staff person if I could do a trick. On the Thursday, I actually did a 10-minute show for everyone. I got a letter last week from Glenwarren Lodge thanking me for the show I did.

It was really hard leaving Mom and I have to admit I cried hard. I knew it would be the last time I saw Mom, and we both cried hard. I love her so much and had to see her. When you are 92, you are on borrowed time. I guess we all are when you think about it. I can't wait to get the book done. Mom will be so proud of it, and she will be the first one to get a copy. I will make sure of that. While the tributes from many family members have been left until the end, they are always first with me. I love them all.

Tribute From Family Members

-From Doug Duncan

I remember how very much Bubby loved his family. He is so proud of his children and their accomplishments. He can talk about them for hours. I've always enjoyed our talks, our games of pool, and, yes, his magic!! My children and grandchildren have had the opportunity to watch him perform many times over the years and keep us laughing, especially my oldest grandson, Jack, who thinks being a magician is so cool. Keep performing your magic, Bubby—Nan would be proud!!

> Love ya, Uncle
> Dougie

-Memories of my Brother, Perley by Roger Palmer

Roger Palmer

I remember when we were about nine or ten years old, we would always go swimming just below the dam where we lived. There was a mill there with big long beams that we would dive into the deepest part of the water.

This one day, Barry Sullivan and I were out there and we went to opposite ends of the beam to dive in. We both dove in and collided head on, and I went down deeper into the water. I remember swallowing a lot of water and had gone down two or three times. I remember seeing a bright light and everything seemed beautiful and peaceful. My whole life flashed before me in an instant, and I believe that I was drowning that day. All of a sudden, I could feel someone pulling on me and the next thing I remember, I was on shore choking and gagging. My older brother, Perley, miraculously appeared that day and pulled me out of the water. I would not be here to tell this story had it not been for Perley.

The Life and Times of Perley the Magician 107

The brothers—Perley, Roger and Ivan.

The brothers—Ivan (lft.), Perley, and Roger (rt.).

Perley and I were always adventurous. One time we decided to make our own boat. We got a huge beam about twenty-five feet long and found a couple of old boards for paddles and headed down the river near our home and then realized we were heading into the mouth of a huge river. We got to shore and had to walk all the way back home. It was quite a long walk back, as the river had pulled us down so far, but we made it together, as always.

Growing up, Perley and I played screenball almost every day, and some days we didn't even have a ball. We would get an old empty Carnation milk can. We would take turns jumping on it until it was crushed small enough to play ball.

We grew up poor, but we sure did have a lot of fun. At the end of every day, Perley would ask, "Did you have fun today, Rog?" As far back as I remember, Perley's Number one goal was to make sure people were happy and had lots of fun. It is no surprise to me that Perley ended up doing magic, because it makes people feel happy. He knows that when a person makes another person happy, that person, in return, feels happy. I have gone on several road trips with Perley and have seen the smiling faces of children and adults, and understand why he loves magic so much. Perley and I have worked together in grocery stores for many years in our hometown, and I have watched firsthand how my brother began his magic career and how he has become a professional magician.

Even today, when Perley and I do anything together, we share fun and laughter, and he still asks, "Hey Rog, did you have fun today?" I always say, "Yeah, I sure did." I am very thankful and proud to be Perley's brother.

Roger Palmer

-Memories of Perley by Brother Ivan

Hello, my name is Ivan Palmer, the younger brother of Perley. First of all, I call him Bubby because it is the only name I have ever known him by.

Bubby started working at Sobeys on Queen Street after he quit school. Later on, our middle brother, Roger, began working at that store, and then when I was in high school around 1965-1966, I worked at the same store. So, there were three Palmers working there at the same time. It was quite something back in the day–first of all, to have a job, and to be working with my brothers. Those are the good times I remember.

Perley always liked good looking old cars and he still does. When he was in his early 20s, he bought this big old blue 1953 Cadillac convertible. He also liked to speed and, yes, he still does ☺. Perley was driving across the old Fredericton bridge late one night and he had secured the top as well as he could. While driving at a top speed across the old bridge, the clasps gave way and the top blew up and ripped apart. To make matters worse, it was October, and one morning he got up to go to work, and the car was full of snow. There are many more car stories, but this is the one I will never forget.

Ivan and family

Over the years, Perley loved softball and played on many teams and won a number of championships. He loved pool and, while very competitive, he was always good natured and loved to have fun, no matter what sport or really anything he worked at. That is my brother, Perley.

One last story: My wife is from Ontario, and the name "Perley" was foreign to her. On one of our trips back to Fredericton, we found Perley living on Perley Avenue in Marysville, which is right beside the Perley Woods. Now what are the chances of that? Perley seemed to be able to make anything happen—I love my big brother, Perley, the magician.

Love
Ivan

-Message From Kelly Palmer, Kim, Perley's Youngest Daughter

My name is Kelly Palmer Kim, Perley's youngest daughter.

    My earliest memories are of being with my dad. I remember going to the baseball park to watch him play. The smell of a baseball field always brings me back to that time. Dad never let me near the dugout because the other players swore and smoked. When I was nine years old, he registered me for little league. I remember us going shopping for my first glove and he was so excited. Of course, I was terrible, but he always encouraged me. Later when I was older and playing in adult leagues, Dad always asked me about the condition of my glove. His main concern was that I had a decent glove to play baseball with. I'm still using the one he bought me 20 years ago. As recently as last summer, Dad still pitched hard enough to make my hand sting. Dad was such a good pitcher; I'm quite certain he could have been professional if he'd had more support. I remember driving with my dad. In the years before car seats and belts, I laid across the bench seat with my head on his lap and went to sleep. Of course, he would be singing. I'm quite similar in that way—always singing.

Kelly Kim

Kelly's husmand Ill with Giju, Hanju and Garam

Dad loves the old country music, and he would always belt out songs in the car. It's still what we do when I visit him and we always take turns singing in the car. He was the only person patient enough to teach me how to drive. Even though I took a lot of sharp turns, he never showed his apprehension and gave me gentle advice—nerves of steel, that guy.

I'm very proud of my dad and what he has done with his life. He always helps people out. He always has time for his friends. More than that, I admire his attitude. He never gets upset by small annoyances. Things that would drive other people crazy, he just lets things roll off his back. I don't think I have ever seen my dad angry or even frustrated. He focuses on the positive and likes to laugh and have fun. I feel like I am similar to him in this, and I'm grateful for his donation of cheerful DNA. When people ask me what my dad does for a living, I say, "He makes people happy." What a great job to have!

Now that Dad is sick, I admire him more than ever. In my opinion, positive attitude and refusal to slow down is aiding him in his fight against cancer. I hope that if I ever find myself in his position, I will follow his inspirational example and remain positive.

Kelly

-A Tribute to Dad From Faye

Perley Palmer—Well, what can I personally write about this guy, my dad who everyone knows. I could write about how warm, funny, and loving he is, but everyone knows that about him already.

(L-R) Faye, Val and Kelly

I guess what I would like to share and honestly, I am not sure if he wants this known, but to me it is one of the things I most admire about him. When my dad was growing up, he had a terrible childhood: He had to leave home at a really early age to work bagging groceries so he could just survive. He had a father that was never kind to him or showed him what love was all about. So many times people grow up to be products of their environments —not my dad though! He never let his past influence the way he treated my brother, sister, or me. Dad never got mad at me that I can ever remember, and trust me he had plenty of opportunities to. I always received love. The only time my dad showed any of us anger was when my brother, the bad kid, dropped the "f" bomb when he was around four, Dad actually spanked him and all the while he was spanking Michael, Dad was crying—he actually cried more than Michael did! That is the one and only time he ever raised a hand to any of us.

I never realized how much I meant to Dad until I had my own child. Dad gave me the greatest gift I could ever receive from a parent and that is the foundation to be a great parent myself and to pass on the love and encouragement that was shown to me from the very beginning.

Faye's daughter Taylor.

Hopefully, when my daughter, Taylor, has her own children, she will be able to pass on Dad's legacy of love that he and my mom and, then later on, he and Val built for us. I am truly a very lucky person to call Perley Palmer my dad.

As I grow older, I find myself forgetting so much of my childhood, but I do remember that Dad worked a lot. He never just sat around–he was always doing something. Whether it was working his job at the grocery store or driving taxi at night, helping out the neighbours with whatever they needed, taking us swimming in the summer in the Saint John River, or skating in the winter at all the ponds out in the backwoods of Sheffield, he was always busy, much to my mom's chagrin, I believe!

There was nothing more fun than my dad sneaking me and my brother, Michael; my sister, Kelly, was too young, across the TransCanada highway to one of the wharves on the river and going swimming: We used to jump off the wharves. Dad would always go first so he would be at the bottom to make sure we came back up! Man, that was thrilling, but I never went without him; I was way too scared to go alone; but with him there, I knew he would always make sure I came back up and was safe.

I used to love going to my dad's softball games at Queens Square, especially at night time when he would play under the lights. He would let me come into the dugout and keep score for the team. I loved watching him play. He was just an amazing pitcher. It was funny because his pitching arm used to be twice the size of his other one.

One of the worst times in my life was when I was around 14 and my mom and dad got divorced. It was terrible and for the longest time I blamed my dad. I know now that he sacrificed so much for us kids so that we could stay with Mom: It must have been terrible for him. I was always angry with him and never really wanted much to do with him. But whenever I needed him, no matter how unkind I was to him, he was always there for me.

When I was in my early 20s, I decided to go back to school and moved in with my dad and Val. By this time, I got over my anger at the divorce and just concentrated on getting to know Dad all over again: It was a fantastic experience for me. Of course, Dad welcomed me into his house with open and loving arms as though all the times I was mean to him never happened. I don't think he will ever know how grateful I am to him for allowing me to get to know him all over again. I remember he used to bring me ice cream every night while I studied; he always cut up bananas in it for me because nothing is better than bananas and ice cream! Actually, people may not know this, but I think my dad could live off of ice cream alone! It is his favourite thing to eat.

I could write pages and pages about how great he is. The thing I want people to know most is that I just simply love my dad with everything I have in my heart.

Love
Faye

For my Dad, Perley Palmer—From Perley's Only Son, Michael

My name is Michael Palmer and I am Perley's only son. I am writing some memorable thoughts and things I remember growing up with my dad.

Dad included me in everything, I was like his left hand and he took me everywhere he could. We used to take our garbage to the dump every week, which was about 10 miles away. Dad had bought me a BB gun and I was allowed to shoot bottles and stuff at the dump. We would spend a lot of time shooting at targets and stuff. The best part was that he would let me drive the car out the dump road. Keep in mind, most of the cars he had were junk. Dad taught me how to drive when I was eight years old and he put pads under the seat so I could look up over the dash because I was so small. By the time I was nine or ten years old, I got so good, he would let me drive the car on the dump road and up to the highway and back. This was the highlight of the week for me. He also taught me how to drive a standard shift and how to do good burnouts.

Perley's son Michael and his wife Linda.

Michael and his son with Perley.

I was around nine years old or so, and one of the fondest memories I have of Dad was going fishing. He had this special spot we called "Old Faithful" down by the Durham Bridge. Dad promised me every time that we would catch a trout and, boy, he didn't lie. Dad and I fished that old spot many times; I even got him to put the worm on my hook for me. We would sit on a log, cast out our line and just wait for the bites, and we always pulled fish out of that spot. As a young boy, the best memory was going to "Old Faithful" with Papa.

In the 70s, we lived in a small house in the Saint John River valley and we didn't have much money to spare. It was a really small community and I only had two friends to hang out with. They came from families that had lots of money and always had nice things like minibikes and ski doos. Our family was simply trying to heat the house and didn't have any money to spare. Dad had got this motorbike (somehow) and it was a Suzuki GS550. I think he got it from a friend and he drove it for a while and loved it. I was with Dad at a motorbike shop in Oromocto and I saw this minibike, it was a Suzuki DS80 and I remember it was almost $600 new. I fell in love with that minibike and asked him if I could have it. He told me we couldn't afford it. Dad watched me jump on the back of my buddy's minibikes to go driving. I know he wished I could have my own. Dad sold the bike he loved and had just enough to go and buy me the bike I wanted for my birthday. I was so happy just knowing how hard it was to get that kind of cash! He made the sacrifice for me and I will never forget that.

Dad has always been a big baseball fan and was a great softball pitcher. As a young boy, he taught me how to play and took me to all of his games. I ended up being the bat boy for the Acadia Marble team, which was one of the teams he played on. There was an RCMP officer at one of Dad's biggest games. He had a radar gun and clocked Dad pitching at 88 miles per hour. I thought, wow, that is fast for a small man like my dad.

Dad and I would go to the ballpark all the time and it would just be the two of us. He taught me how to pitch, catch, and bat. Dad spent countless hours practicing with me. I got better at ball and he came to all my games to cheer me on and eventually got to see me pitch a no-hitter. I remember that last pitch, and how proud Dad was of me. It was really special because it is a memory we both share and something that I will never forget.

In 1973, my other two buddies played hockey and I wanted to try hard to play like them. I was a really small kid and looked and felt out of place. Dad took me to the rink and registered me for hockey.

We went to the first game of the season and I was really bad. I had a hard time skating and I remember that during the practice, I fell down really hard and hurt my head. Dad came down to the ice and picked me up; he knew that I was really struggling out there. The funny thing is, as a Dad now; I can see how he must have felt watching his little boy out there falling apart. My dad picked me up and he said, "Son, if you don't want to play, you do not have to." On the drive home, he told me it may be a good idea to go out again and try it. I didn't want to, but I took his advice and, before the end of that season, I was the captain of the team. Dad taught me never to quit.

Dad always was a great athlete and was good at pretty much any sport. He taught me at a young age how to play pool. We had an old wooden pool table in the cellar of our home. Dad and I would spend hours playing with Uncle Roger, and I loved it! However, I had a really hard time beating him because I was only a child. As I got older, I continued to play pool and won many tournaments. However, to this day, for some reason, I can beat anyone in pool—except Dad!!

In 1977, I was with Dad, when he was helping a new member in our community drill their well. It was what all the men in the neighborhood did as a welcoming present. I was only nine years old and too young to help so I sat on a tractor and watched the grown-ups. It was a homemade tower built out of wood and held together by wires. I was watching the men pull a rope and drop it to pound the stake in the ground when I witnessed something terrible. One of the wires broke free, the whole tower fell striking Dad on the head, then throwing him into the rim of the tractor I was sitting on. The wound to his head was so massive I actually saw his brain pulsing. I really thought Dad was going to die that day—I was never so terrified. However, he healed and it proved, once again, just how strong my dad is.

Living in the Saint John River Valley was scary in the spring. In 1979, we had a tremendous amount of flooding. I remember the river got so high, it was actually level with the highway. I was sitting in the front yard and I said, "Hey, Papa, will that water come over the road?" He said, "Don't worry, Mikey." About 4 a.m., he woke me up. Dad carried me and my sisters out to the front lawn, where he had a rubber boat tied to a tree and put us in it. The water had flooded right into the house. Dad and our neighbor, Mr. Forbes, worked frantically to secure everything—chickens, pigs, you name it. We ended up staying at Tibbits Hall at the UNB campus for about 4 weeks. My sisters and Mom stayed in one dorm, Dad and I stayed in another. Every night, he sang to me and made me feel like everything was going to be OK, and it was!

In 1979, my parents got divorced. Mom moved us to Halifax and we couldn't see Dad much. As a young child, it was hard for me to understand why all this happened, but Dad always told me, "Son, someday I will tell you all about it." As time went on and I had a child of my own, I truly understood the pain he must have been going through. Throughout the years, Dad was always there for me.

In 1986, I started my first real job. I was working full time earning five bucks an hour and always had a hard time making ends meet. I was driving a car that wasn't fit for the road and it finally died. I needed a car to get to work and I had absolutely no credit. I saw this 1980 Camaro for sale and they wanted $3,800. It was a dream car to me! I called my dad and said, "Papa, can you help me out." I knew he didn't have the cash, but I thought he could help and did he ever! He knew a friend that worked at a bank and Dad co-signed a loan for me. I paid it all back; I couldn't have done it without Dad's help. He always did what he could to help me more times than I could count.

My dad has always been there for me no matter what. When you are young, you don't seem to understand it, but, as you get older and have your own children, you finally do. Dad taught me to play ball, pool, hockey, swim, drive, shoot, and manage money. The one thing Dad taught me most of all was how to be a good person. I have learned from his example about treating people nice and being good to people.

Love,
Michael

-Tribute From Pastor Theo Craig

I have known Perley for the better part of 35 years. I remember when he first started coming around. He drove into the yard with an old beat-up car smashed in on one side. I thought you must be kidding! He was going to take my mom out on a date in that old rattletrap. But, like with most things with Perley, things were not always as they appeared. It didn't take long to realize this man was caring and protective to my mother and, for that, I have been forever grateful.

Perley always had to have a project; he could never sit still for long. He made clocks in the shed and then sold pictures in the mall. It was around this time, he began to experiment with doing some magic tricks— eventually he found that doing tricks was easy.

He has packed my mother up and moved her from house to house all over Fredericton for the past 22 years. They would get a house all comfortable and

Theo–top (lft.), wife Cheryl–bottom (lft.) & family.

then she would want to sell. He had more patience than many men would have had when it came to her desire to move.

One great thing about Perley is that he was never a fault finder and always tried to steer clear of saying negative things about people. I think that is a wonderful thing. Even through his sickness, he has remained upbeat and positive—he has surrounded himself with people who are not always feeling sorry for themselves.

Being around Perley can be humorous to say the least. Sometimes he would get himself into some funny and awkward situations and then, as he retold the story, it would become bigger than life. We all love Perley–not because he is so great or does magic, but because he is real without pretention. He is who he is and that is enough: He is an uncomplicated man who truly loves life and people.

Theo's granddaughter Gabrielle, daughter Ashley, and husband Rick

I'm thankful, most of all that Perley has loved Mom and they have had a wonderful life together. For that, I will always love and appreciate Perley.

Theo Craig

-Tribute to my Dad, Perley, the Magician from Pat Price

I can't remember what year Perley came into my life; I suppose I was 15 or 16 when he and Mom got together. Prior to that, I didn't have a positive male influence in my life, with the exception of my uncles, whom I did not often see.

When I met Perley, I had no idea how he would shape my life and help me to become a better human being. I didn't anticipate that he would teach me how to be a young woman nor did I anticipate how much I would love him. He's kind of grown on me over the years.

We've had moments where I have been rebellious and he has held me accountable. There have been times when I did not want to follow his advice and may have even resented him giving it to me. Throughout it all, he has loved me patiently and encouraged me to do better. He has become my dad in the truest sense of the word. He never allowed me to get away with murder and I always knew when he disapproved of a choice.

Pat Price

Valerie and daughter, Pat.

Valerie with Pat's family.

He spent time talking with me and supporting me. He could be firm when necessary, but also knew the power of laughter and when to let things go. People refer to him as a magic man and he is. He certainly gave me magic. I never anticipated having the relationship that we do, and how he has brought our family together.

I was here in Fredericton when Perley was diagnosed with cancer. His other children didn't live in the city. I naturally went with Perley and Mom to get the diagnosis and the prognosis from the oncologist. I sent a letter to all the family explaining the details of what the doctor had said.

I can't imagine my life without Perley. He isn't my biological father, but he is the best Dad in the world. He took a broken little girl and loved her. Perley's magic healed me and helped me to become the woman I am. I love you, Perley.

Love,
Pat

Pat and grandson Palmer

Perley – Experiencing Generosity

While the last year has been different, Valerie and I have continued to enjoy our family and we are overwhelmed by the generosity of our friends and our community. This last summer we enjoyed a wonderful trip and were grateful to have an RV given to us for the trip.

Our Blessings—Valerie

While the last year has been different, we have continued to enjoy our family and we are overwhelmed by the generosity of our friends and our community. This last summer, we enjoyed a wonderful trip and were grateful to have an RV given to us for the trip by our good friend Dave.

Valerie

Tribute by Dave-RV World

I came to Fredericton early in the 1990s and often heard of a guy with an ability to mesmerize children with his sleight-of-hand tricks and larger than life personality. I believe we first reached out to him with an invite to entertain the attendees at our annual RV show almost 20 years ago. What was wonderful was the friendship that developed between Perley and I as the years progressed.

Perley possessed the sleight-of-hand abilities of a magician: He personified the definition of living life with a positive attitude. His smile and bubbly personality can make a stressful situation seem unimportant! Perley moved from being a provider of a service to our company to a customer many times over. Over time he became a treasured friend of both myself and RV fellow co-workers. Perley always treats each one of us with the utmost respect and never leaves without offering us a trick of some kind that always left us wondering "How did he do that?!".

When asked to write a couple of paragraphs about my dealings with Perley, I was honored. I hadn't seen him for a few months, but had been aware of his diagnosis. One early morning, I was at the local hospital for blood work when I heard his familiar voice from one of the cubicles explaining to the hospital interviewer, one of very few Frederictonians that didn't know him, "I'm Perley. " I imagine that probably followed with him finding a card in his pocket or a coin behind his ear, but I couldn't see the interaction and was just barely able to hear the conversation. When he got up to move to the next station, I was shocked to see that he looked frail and had some hair loss from his chemo treatments. I immediately went over to say, "Hi" and asked how he was doing. Perley flat out told me "Great! I have had a blessed life, Dave." He told me that you wouldn't see any tears from him as there were a lot of people worse off than him. I gave him a hug and told him he was an inspiration to all of us. Both he and I, two grown men, shed a tear that morning.

I have seen him many times since and, once again, the power of his positivity has helped him move through some difficult times. One of Perley's bucket list items was to tour Cape Breton and, thankfully, we could help him knock that one off his list last summer. I hope we have an opportunity to help knock off more items on his list in the years ahead of us.

Your friend,
Dave Dobson

"Dr. Bonnie" Reflects

I know that Perley is so humble: He would never want the attention to be on him, but on others. As his good buddy, Bob, says, "Perley is a pearl and a gem and he is fondly known as the People's Mayor." This appears to be true and has been exemplified in the book by Perley's many friends and his family. This memory from Perley's only son, Michael, describes the true heart of Perley: integrity, dignity, and gratitude. Perley has a wonderful family and so many "true" friends and a family that has learned to love from a man who has a heart of gold. Perley continues to be a blessing to so many.

A Lifelong Lesson Learned: Michael Palmer

In the mid-70s, Dad had to keep animals, because it helped put food on the table. We had a chicken coop that housed about 25 chickens. Every so often, those chickens would lay eggs and hatch babies. I would love it when that happened. However, many times, the rats would get into the coop and eat the eggs or even worse the baby chicks. One day, Dad and I went to the coop to find that rats had destroyed a lot of eggs and some baby chicks. We saw this little premature chick that was laying there barely alive. Dad took that little chick into the cellar and we made a tiny house out of a shoe box filled with hay, then put a light bulb over it to keep the chick warm. Dad fed it with an eye dropper with sugar and water. We spent a few weeks nursing the little chick back to life; I remember finally the chick was big enough to go back with the others. We ended up naming it, "Miracle Chicken." This was a great lesson for me: There have been so many more since that day.

My dad is the best example I could ever imagine. Now, more than ever, Dad is proving just how strong he actually is. My dad was and will be—always, my hero.

Dreams Come True: Facing Life Hand in Hand—Valerie

In March 2016, Perley and I realized a dream come true when we went to Oahu, Hawaii, for 13 days. This was a huge breath of fresh air in both of our lives, and we pray that God will grant us another reset and that we continue on this wonderful adventure and life that we have created. We both know that this will be of God's will and not our own. We have faith and trust in the outcome in this part of our journey.

Perley and I have done a lot of wonderful things together throughout our 32 plus years. We are blessed to have each other and, between us, we have five children, 14 grandchildren, and seven great grandchildren, along with many relatives and friends.

The cancer diagnosis has been hard on both of us. Our church family and our faith in God are what brought us through to this point. We are holding on to every anchor as we take each step of each waking day. Perley is so blessed to have so many people praying for his total healing: This gives us comfort. We love and appreciate each prayer and person who is praying for us. We trust God who is watching over us as we travel this rocky road together.

We are not sure about the future, but then who is? I know that whatever happens, Perley and I will face this challenge—together—hand in hand.

Perley and Valerie

Conclusion

Just like Perley was loved and nurtured in a shoe box from his birth, he knows deep in his heart and soul that love never left him. He has done unto others what was done unto him—show love. Perley is the miracle man that we all love and the show must go on.

All proceeds from this book will go directly to Perley, The Magician.

References

Fraser, E. (2015, July 14). It's no trick—city names July 13 as Perley Palmer Day. *The Daily Gleaner*. Retrieved from https://www.telegraphjournal.com/telegraph-journal/story/49363942/?nopromo=1

Something beautiful. (n.d.). Retrieved from http://www.allthelyrics.com/lyrics/gaither_vocal_band/something_beautiful-lyrics-213205.html

What does a magician do? (n.d.). *What is a magician?* Retrieved from https://www.sokanu.com/careers/magician/

Perley's front cover picture. Source: *The magic of Perley*. (n.d.), Photographer Brian Smith for the New Brunswick Provincial Exhibition. Retrieved from http://www.nbex.ca/perley-the-magician

Billy Saunders–NB SPORTS HOF ALUMNI and OLYMPIAN Monica Hitchcock with Perley

Perley and Ron

Perley and Glen Chase

Valerie and Theo

Perley and Elliot

Christian and Valerie

Grampy with Aiden and Lily

Perley and Bob Kenny

Amy and Perley

Janelle, Addie and Piper

Perley and Valerie

Evelyn with the family

Theo's daughter Ashley and Nick

Daniel

Granddaughter Juliana, husband Jeremy, son Jaxon, nephews Nolan and Liam

Sisters

Michael and Girls

Grandson Jeremy and wife Jessica

Toronto Blue Jays
Joe Carter and Perley

Matt Stairs and Perley

Perley always on the move

Valerie, Pat and family

Perley, Val and Baby Palmer

Bob Dewar and Perley

Ron, Val, Bill, Roger

Perley, Ivan, and grandchildren

Joe Fisher, long time friend of Perley